HEAVEN
II

"And the twelve gates were twelve pearls;
each one of the gates was a single pearl.
And the street of the city was pure gold,
like transparent glass."
(Revelation 21:21)

HEAVEN II

Filled With God's Glory

DR. JAEROCK LEE

URIM BOOKS

HEAVEN II : FILLED WITH GOD'S GLORY
by Dr. Jaerock Lee
Published by Urim Books (Representative: Seongkeon Vin)
235-3, Guro-dong 3, Guro-gu, Seoul, Korea
www.urimbooks.com

Previously published in Korean by Urim Books, Seoul, Korea.

First Published September 2004
Second Edition April 2009
Third Edition August 2009
Fourth Edition December 2011
Fifth Edition April 2018

Edited by Dr. Geumsun Vin
Designed by Editorial Bureau of Urim Books
Printed by VST
For more information contact at urimbook@hotmail.com

Preface

Praying that you may become God's true child and share true love in eternal happiness and joy in New Jerusalem, where the love of God abounds...

I give all thanks and glory to Father God, who has clearly revealed to me the life in heaven, and blessed us to publish *Heaven I: As Clear and Beautiful as Crystal,* and now *Heaven II: Filled with God's Glory.*

I had longed to know about heaven in detail, and kept on praying and fasting. After seven years, God finally answered my prayers and today, He is revealing deeper secrets about the spiritual realm.

In the first of the two-part *Heaven* series, I briefly introduced the various dwelling places in heaven, categorizing them into Paradise, the First Kingdom, the Second Kingdom, the Third Kingdom, and New Jerusalem. The second will explore in greater detail the most beautiful and glorious dwelling place of all within heaven, New Jerusalem.

The God of love showed New Jerusalem to the apostle John and allowed him to record it in the Bible. Today, as the Lord's Advent is ever so near, God is pouring out the Holy Sprit on countless people and revealing heaven in the greatest detail. This is so that nonbelievers all over the world will come to believe in the afterlife that consists of heaven and hell, and that those who confess their belief in Christ will lead victorious lives in Him and endeavor to spread the gospel all around the globe.

This is why the apostle Paul, who was in charge of spreading the gospel to the Gentiles, admonished his spiritual son Timothy, saying, *"But you, be sober in all things, endure hardship, do the work of an evangelist, fulfill your ministry"* (2 Timothy 4:5).

God revealed clearly to me heaven and hell so that I would spread the account of ages to come to the four corners of the world. God wants all people to receive salvation; He does not want to see even a single soul falling into hell. All the more, God wants as many people as possible to enter and dwell perpetually in New Jerusalem.

Thus, no one ought to judge or condemn these God-given messages revealed through the inspiration of the Holy Spirit.

In *Heaven II* you will find a great deal of secrets concerning heaven, such as the appearance of God who has existed from prior to the beginning of time, the throne of God, and the like.

I believe that such details and accounts will provide all those people who earnestly desire heaven with a tremendous amount of happiness and joy.

The City of New Jerusalem, constructed by an immeasurable love and astonishing power of God, is filled with His glory. In New Jerusalem are the spiritual summit at which God formed Himself into the Trinity in order to carry out the human cultivation, and the very throne of God. Can you imagine how magnificent, beautiful, and bright the entire place would be? It is such a fantastic and holy site that no human wisdom can possibly fathom it!

Therefore, you must realize that New Jerusalem is not rewarded to all those who receive salvation. Instead, it is given only to God's children whose hearts, after having been cultivated in this world for a long time, have come forth as pure and clear as crystal.

I give special thanks to Geumsun Vin, Director of Editorial Bureau and the staff, and Translation Bureau in this publication.

I bless in the name of the Lord that whoever reads this book may become God's true child and share true love in eternal happiness and joy in New Jerusalem that is filled with God's glory!

Jaerock Lee

# Introduction

Hoping that you may be blessed as you find out in the most lucid detail about New Jerusalem, and dwell in eternity as close as you can to the throne of God in heaven...

I give all thanks and glory to God, who has blessed us to publish *Heaven I: As Clear and Beautiful as Crystal* and now its sequel, *Heaven II: Filled with God's Glory.*

This book consists of nine chapters, all of which provide a clear description of the holiest and most beautiful dwelling place in heaven, New Jerusalem, in terms of its size, splendor, and life therein.

Chapter 1, "New Jerusalem: Filled with God's Glory," provides an overview of New Jerusalem and explains such secrets as the throne of God and the summit of the spiritual realm, at which God formed Himself into the Trinity.

Chapter 2, "Names of the Twelve Tribes and Twelve Apostles," explains the outer appearance of the City of New Jerusalem. It is surrounded by tall and enormous walls, and the names of the Twelve Tribes of Israel are inscribed on the City's twelve gates on all four sides. On the twelve foundations of the City are the names of the Twelve Apostles, and the reason and significance of each inscription will be clarified.

In Chapter 3, "The Size of New Jerusalem," you will discover the appearance and the dimension of New Jerusalem. This chapter explains why God measures the size of New Jerusalem with golden reed and that in order to enter and dwell in this City, one must possess all the pertinent spiritual qualifications, measured by the golden reed. It also discusses why the width, length, and height of the City of New Jerusalem is 6,000 Ri, respectively, in the traditional Korean measure.

Chapter 4, "Made of Pure Gold and Jewels of All Colors," explores in detail each material with which the City of New Jerusalem is built. The entire City is decorated with pure gold and other precious stones, and the chapter describes the beauty of their colors, glitter, and lights. Furthermore, by explaining the reason God adorned the walls of the City with jasper and the entire New Jerusalem with pure gold that is as clear as glass, the chapter also discusses the importance of spiritual faith.

In Chapter 5, "The Significances of the Twelve Foundations," you will learn about the walls of New Jerusalem, built on twelve foundations, and the beauty and spiritual significance of jasper, sapphire, chalcedony; emerald, sardonyx; sardius, chrysolite, beryl, topaz, chrysoprase, jacinth, and amethyst. When you add up the spiritual significance of each of the twelve jewels, you will notice the heart of Jesus Christ and the heart of God. The chapter encourages you to accomplish the hearts symbolized by the twelve jewels so that you may enter and eternally dwell in the City of New Jerusalem.

Chapter 6, "The Twelve Pearl Gates and the Golden Road," explains the reasons and spiritual significance of God's making of the twelve gates of pearl, as well as the spiritual meaning of the golden road that is as clear as glass. Just as a shell produces a precious pearl after it endures great pain, the chapter encourages you to run towards the Twelve Gates of Pearl of New Jerusalem by overcoming all kinds of hardships and trials in faith and with hope.

Chapter 7, "The Charming Spectacle," takes you inside the city walls of New Jerusalem that is always brightly lit. You will learn the spiritual significance of the phrase, "God and the Lamb are its temple," the size and beauty of the castle in which the Lord resides, and the glory of the people who will enter New Jerusalem to spend the eternity with the Lord.

Chapter 8, "I Saw the Holy City, New Jerusalem," introduces to you the house of an individual, among many who will have led faithful and sanctified lives on the earth, who is to receive great rewards in heaven. You will be able to catch a glimpse of the happy days that lie ahead in New Jerusalem by reading about various sizes and splendor of heavenly houses, many kinds of facilities, and overall life in heaven.

The ninth and final Chapter, "The First Banquet in New Jerusalem," takes you to the scene of the first banquet to be held in New Jerusalem after the Judgment of the Great White Throne. With the introduction of some of the forefathers of faith who dwell close to God's throne, Heaven II concludes by blessing each reader to have a heart that is as pure and clear as crystal so that he/she may be able to dwell closer to the throne of God in New Jerusalem.

The more you learn about heaven, the more wondrous it becomes. New Jerusalem, which can be considered the "nucleus" of heaven, is where you will find God's throne. If you know about the beauty and glory of New Jerusalem, you will surely and earnestly hope for heaven and be clear-minded about your life in Christ.

As the time of Jesus' return, before which He will have finished preparing dwelling places in heaven for us, is extremely near today, with *Heaven II: Filled with God's Glory* I hope that you will prepare for the eternal life as well.

I pray in the name of the Lord Jesus Christ that you will be able to dwell close to God's throne by sanctifying yourself with the fervent hope of life in New Jerusalem and being faithful in all your God-given duties.

Geumsun Vin,
Director of Editorial Bureau

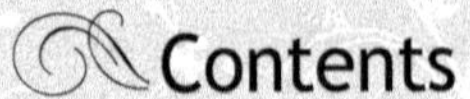# Contents

Preface

Introduction

Chapter 1

New Jerusalem:
Filled with God's Glory

"And he carried me away in the Spirit
to a great and high mountain,
and showed me the holy city, Jerusalem,
coming down out of heaven from God,
having the glory of God.
Her brilliance was like a very costly stone,
as a stone of crystal-clear jasper."

- Revelation 21:10-11

Heaven is a realm in the four-dimensional world, ruled by the God of love and justice Himself. Even though it is not visible to the naked eyes, heaven surely exists. How much happiness, joy, thanksgiving, and glory would be overflowing in heaven since it is the best gift God has prepared for His children who have received salvation?

Yet, there are different dwelling places within heaven. There is New Jerusalem in which is God's throne, and there is also Paradise where people barely saved are to stay perpetually. Just as life in a hut and life in the castle of a king vary significantly even on this earth, there is much difference in glory between entering Paradise and entering New Jerusalem.

Nevertheless, some believers consider "heaven" and "New Jerusalem" the same, and some of them do not even know that there is New Jerusalem. How pitiful this is! It is not easy to possess heaven even if you know about it. How, then, can one advance to New Jerusalem without knowing about it?

Therefore, God revealed New Jerusalem to the apostle John and let him write about it in detail in the Bible. Revelation 21 explains New Jerusalem in depth, and John was moved just by looking at the exterior of it.

He confessed in Revelation 21:10-11, *"And he carried me away in the Spirit to a great and high mountain, and showed me the holy city, Jerusalem, coming down out of heaven from God, having the glory of God. Her brilliance was like a very costly stone, as a stone of crystal-clear jasper."*

Why, then, is New Jerusalem full of God's glory?

In New Jerusalem is God's Throne

In New Jerusalem is the throne of God. How full of God's glory would New Jerusalem be since God Himself dwells in it?

That is why you can see that people are giving glory, thanks, and honor to God day and night in Revelation 4:8: *"And the four living creatures, each one of them having six wings, are full of eyes around and within; and day and night they do not cease to say, 'Holy, holy, holy is the Lord God, the Almighty, who was and who is and who is to come.'"*

New Jerusalem is also called the "Holy City" because it is made anew with the Word of God, who is truthful, blameless, and the light itself without any darkness found in Him.

Jerusalem is the place where Jesus, who came in flesh to open the way of salvation for all mankind, preached the gospel and fulfilled the Law with love. Therefore, God built New Jerusalem for all believers who fulfilled the Law with love to stay.

God's throne at the center of New Jerusalem

Then, where in New Jerusalem is God's throne? The answer is revealed to us in Revelation 22:3-4:

There will no longer be any curse; and the throne of God and of the Lamb will be in it, and His bond-servants will serve Him; they will see His face, and His name will be on their foreheads.

The throne of God is located at the center of New Jerusalem, and only those who obey God's Word like an obedient servant can enter there and see the face of God.

This is because God has told us in Hebrews 12:14, *"Pursue peace with all men, and the sanctification without which no one will see the Lord,"* and in Matthew 5:8, *"Blessed are the pure in heart, for they shall see God."* Therefore, you ought to realize that not everybody can enter New Jerusalem that houses God's throne.

What does the throne of God look like? Some may think that it only looks like a big chair, but that is not so. In a narrow sense, it stands for a seat on which God sits, but in a broad sense, it refers to the dwelling place of God.

Thus, "God's throne" refers to the dwelling place of God, and around His throne at the center of New Jerusalem, are rainbows and thrones of the twenty-four elders.

Rainbows and thrones of the twenty-four elders

You can feel the beauty, magnificence, and size of the throne of God in Revelation 4:3-6:

> *And He who was sitting was like a jasper stone and a sardius in appearance; and there was a rainbow around the throne, like an emerald in appearance. Around the throne were twenty-four thrones; and upon the thrones I saw twenty-four elders sitting, clothed in white garments, and golden crowns on their heads. Out from the throne come flashes of lightning and sounds and peals of thunder. And there were seven lamps of fire burning before the throne, which are the seven Spirits of God; and before the throne there was something like a sea of glass, like crystal; and in the center and around the throne, four living creatures full of eyes in front and behind..*

Many angels and heavenly hosts are serving God. There are also many other spiritual creatures such as cherubim and the four living creatures that are guarding Him.

Also, the sea of glass is spread out before the throne of God. The sight of it is so beautiful, with many kinds of lights that surround the throne of God reflected on the sea of glass.

How do the twenty-four elders surround the throne of God? Twelve of them are located behind the Lord, and the other twelve behind the Holy Spirit. These twenty-four elders are sanctified individuals and have the right to testify before God.

The throne of God is so beautiful, magnificent, and great beyond any human imagination.

The Original Throne of God

Acts 7:55-56 recounts Stephen's seeing of the throne of the Lamb on the right side of God's throne:

But being full of the Holy Spirit, [Stephen] gazed intently into heaven and saw the glory of God, and Jesus standing at the right hand of God; and he said, 'Behold, I see the heavens opened up and the Son of Man standing at the right hand of God.''

Stephen became a martyr by being stoned while he was boldly preaching Jesus Christ. Just before Stephen died, his spiritual eyes opened and he could see the Lord standing on the right side of God's throne. The Lord could not remain seated knowing that Stephen would soon become a martyr by the Jews who had listened to his message. So the Lord stood up from His throne and shed tears watching Stephen stoned to death, and Stephen saw this scene with his opened spiritual eyes.

Likewise, Stephen saw God's throne where God and the Lord stay, and you should realize that this throne is different from the one that the apostle John saw in New Jerusalem. The throne of God Stephen saw is the original throne of God.

In old days, when the king left his palace to look around the country and the people, his staff built a place that resembled a palace for the king to stay temporarily. In the same way, God's throne in New Jerusalem is not the throne where God usually stays, but the one where He stays for short periods of time.

The original throne of God in the beginning

God existed alone, embracing the whole universe before the beginning of time (Exodus 3:14; John 1:1; Revelation 22:13). The universe then was not the same as what we are seeing with our eyes now, but was one single space before the division into the spiritual and physical worlds. God existed as the light and shone the whole universe.

He was not a mere beam of light, but existed as such shiny, beautiful lights that were like a flow of water bearing colors of a rainbow. You might understand this better if you think of the Auroras seen around the North Pole. An Aurora is a group of different colors of light spread out like a curtain, and it is said that the sight is so beautiful that whoever sees it once will never forget the beauty of it.

Then, how much more beautiful would the lights of God–who is the Light itself–be, and how can we express the splendor of so many beautiful lights mixed?

That is why it says in 1 John 1:5, *"This is the message we have heard from Him and announce to you, that God is Light, and in Him there is no darkness at all."* The reason it is said that "God is Light" is not only to express the spiritual meaning that God has no darkness at all, but also to describe God's appearance who existed as light before the beginning.

This very God, who before the beginning of time existed alone as the light in the universe, was filled with voice.

God existed as the light filled with voice, and this voice is "the Word" to which John 1:1 alludes: *"In the beginning was the Word, and the Word was with God, and the Word was God."*

In the space where God existed as the light with a chiming

voice, there are separate spaces for the Father, the Son, and the Holy Spirit to stay and rest individually. In the area where there is God's original throne in the space of the beginning, there is a space for rest, rooms to have conversations, and paths for strolls as well.

Only very special angels and those whose hearts resemble God's own heart are allowed in this place. This place is separate, mysterious, and secure. Furthermore, this place that houses the throne of God the Trinity is located in the space where God existed alone in the beginning, and it is in the fourth heaven, separate from New Jerusalem in the third heaven.

The Bride of the Lamb

God wants all people to resemble His heart and enter New Jerusalem. However, He still showed His mercy to those who have not accomplished this level of sanctification through the human cultivation. He divided the kingdom of heaven into many dwelling places from Paradise to the First, Second, and Third Kingdoms of Heaven and rewards His children according to what they have done.

God gives New Jerusalem to His true children who are completely sanctified and have been faithful in all His house. He has built New Jerusalem in remembrance of Jerusalem, the foundation of the gospel, and as a new vessel to contain everything about that they have completed the law with love.

We can read from Revelation 21:2 that God has prepared New Jerusalem so beautifully that the City reminds John of a bride magnificently adorned for her groom:

And I saw the holy city, new Jerusalem, coming down out of heaven from God, made ready as a bride adorned for her husband.

New Jerusalem is like a bride beautifully adorned

God is preparing gorgeous dwelling places in heaven for the brides of the Lord who are preparing themselves beautifully to receive the spiritual bridegroom the Lord Jesus by circumcising their hearts. The most beautiful place among these eternal dwelling places is the City of New Jerusalem.

That is why Revelation 21:9 expresses the City of New Jerusalem, which is most beautifully decorated for the Lord's brides, as *"The bride, the wife of the Lamb."*

How rapturous would New Jerusalem be since it is the best gift for the brides of the Lord that God of love prepared Himself? People will be moved so much when they enter their respective houses, built and cared for by God's love and delicate, detailed considerations. It is because God makes each house perfectly fit the owner's taste.

A bride serves her husband and provides a place for him to rest. In the same sense, the houses in New Jerusalem serve and embrace the brides of the Lord. The place is so comfortable and safe that people are filled with happiness and joy.

In this world, no matter how well a wife serves her husband, she cannot give the perfect peace and joy. However, the houses in New Jerusalem can give peace and joy that people cannot experience in this world because those houses are made to perfectly satisfy the owner's taste. Houses are built beautifully and magnificently according to the owners' tastes because they are for the people whose hearts resemble God's heart. How wondrous and brilliant would they be since the Lord is in charge of the construction?

If you truly believe in heaven, you will be happy just to think about so many angels building heavenly houses with gold and jewels following God's law that rewards each individual according to what one has done.

Can you imagine how much happier and more joyous the life in New Jerusalem, which serves and embraces you like a wife, would be?

Heavenly houses are decorated according to one's deeds

The heavenly houses began to be built ever since our Lord resurrected and ascended into heaven, and they are being built even now according to our deeds. Thus, constructions on the houses of the ones whose lives on this earth have come to an end are completed; the foundations are being laid and pillars are going up for some houses; and the works on some other houses are almost completed.

When all the heavenly houses of the believers are completed, the Lord is to return to the earth but this time in the air:

In My Father's house are many dwelling places; if it were not so, I would have told you; for I go to prepare a place for you. If I go and prepare a place for you, I will come again and receive you to Myself, that where I am, there you may be also. (John 14:2-3)

The eternal dwelling places of the saved people are decided at the Judgment of the White Throne.

When the owner enters his or her house after the dwelling place and rewards have been decided according to each one's measure of faith, the house will then shine completely. It is because the owner and the house makes a perfect pair when the owner enters his or her house just as a husband and a wife become one flesh.

How full of God's glory would New Jerusalem be since it houses the throne of God, and many houses are being built for God's true children who can share true love with Him forever?

Shiny as Bright Jewels and Clear as Crystal

When led by the Holy Spirit, the apostle John was at awe when he saw the Holy City of New Jerusalem, and he could only confess as follows:

And he carried me away in the Spirit to a great and high mountain, and showed me the holy city, Jerusalem, coming down out of heaven from God, having the glory of God. Her brilliance was like a very costly stone, as a stone of crystal-clear jasper (Revelation 21:10-11).

John gave glory to God as he was looking at the magnificent New Jerusalem from the top of a mountain, when led by the Holy Spirit.

New Jerusalem, shining with the glory of God

What does it mean to say that the brilliance of New Jerusalem that shines with the glory of God is "like a very costly stone, as a stone of crystal-clear jasper"? There are many kinds of jewels and they have different names according to their components and colors. To be considered precious, each stone has to give out a very beautiful color. Thus, the expression "like a very costly stone" implies that it is the perfection of beauty. John the apostle compared the beautiful light of New Jerusalem to that of precious stones people consider very valuable and beautiful.

Furthermore, New Jerusalem has enormous and grandiose houses, and is decorated with heavenly jewels that shine rapturous lights, and you can tell the lights are glittering and beautiful even if you look at the City from afar. Bluish, white lights that are resplendent with many colors seem to be embracing New Jerusalem. How impressive and delightful would the sight be?

Revelation 21:18 tells us that the wall of New Jerusalem is made of jasper. Unlike opaque jasper on this earth, the jasper in heaven has a bluish color and is so beautiful and clear that when you look at it, it feels like you are looking into clear water. It is almost impossible to express the beauty of its color with the things of this world. Perhaps it can be compared to a shiny, blue light reflected on clear waves. Moreover, we can only express its color as being clear, bluish, and white. Jasper represents elegance and clearness of God, and God's "righteousness" that is spotless, clear and honest.

There are many kinds of crystal, and in heavenly terms it refers to a colorless, transparent, and hard stone that is as clean and clear as pure water. Clean and clear crystals have been widely used for decoration from old days because they are not only clear and transparent, but also beautifully reflect lights.

Crystal, though not very expensive, splendidly reflects lights to make them look like rainbows. Moreover, God has placed the brilliance of glory on the heavenly crystals with His power, so it cannot even be compared to those found on this earth. John the apostle is attempting to express the beauty, clearness, and resplendence of New Jerusalem with crystal.

The Holy City of New Jerusalem is filled with the wondrous glory of God. How magnificent, beautiful and shiny would New Jerusalem be since it houses the throne of God and the summit where God formed Himself into the Trinity?

Chapter 2

Names of the Twelve Tribes
and Twelve Apostles

"It had a great and high wall, with twelve gates,
and at the gates twelve angels;
and names were written on them,
which are the names of the twelve tribes
of the sons of Israel.
There were three gates on the east
and three gates on the north
and three gates on the south
and three gates on the west.
And the wall of the city had twelve foundation stones,
and on them were the twelve names
of the twelve apostles of the Lamb."

- Revelation 21:12-14

New Jerusalem is surrounded by walls that shine brilliant and glittering lights. Everyone's jaw will drop to the floor at the size, magnificence, beauty, and glory of these walls.

The City is cube-shaped and has three gates on each side: east, west, north, and south. It has a total of twelve gates and is unimaginably massive. A dignified and majestic angel guards each gate and the names of the twelve tribes are inscribed on these gates.

Also around the walls of New Jerusalem are twelve foundations on which twelve pillars stand and the names of the twelve disciples are recorded. Everything in New Jerusalem is made with the number 12, the number of light, as its basis. This is to help everyone easily understand that New Jerusalem is the place for those children of light whose hearts resemble the heart of God, who Himself is the light.

Let us now look at the reasons twelve angels are guarding the twelve gates of New Jerusalem and the names of the twelve tribes and twelve apostles are recorded all over the City.

Twelve Angels Guard the Gates

In old days, many soldiers or guards kept watch of the gates of castles in which the kings or other high officials stayed and lived. This measure was necessary to protect the buildings from enemies and intruders. Yet, twelve angels are guarding the gates of New Jerusalem even though no one can enter or invade as he wishes because the City houses God's throne. What, then, is the reason?

To express the riches, authority, and glory

The City of New Jerusalem is enormous and grandiose beyond our imagination. The great Forbidden City of China in which emperors used to live is just as big as an individuals' house in New Jerusalem. Even the size of the Great Wall of China, one of the Seven Wonders of the Ancient World, cannot be compared to that of the City of New Jerusalem.

The first reason there are twelve angels guarding the gates is to symbolize the riches and honor, authority, and glory. Even today, the powerful or the wealthy have their private guards in and around their houses, and this shows the richness and the authority of the residents.

Thus, it is obvious that angels in higher positions guard the gates of the City of New Jerusalem that houses God's throne. One can feel the authority of God and New Jerusalem residents at a glance just by looking at the twelve angels, whose presence adds to the beauty and glory of New Jerusalem itself.

To protect God's recognized children

What, then, is the second reason that twelve angels guard the gates of New Jerusalem? Hebrews 1:14 asks, *"Are they not all ministering spirits, sent out to render service for the sake of those who will inherit salvation?"* God protects His children living on this earth with His blazing eyes and the angels sent by Him. Thus, those who live according to God's Word will not be slandered by Satan but be protected from tests, troubles, natural and man-made disasters, diseases, and accidents.

Also, there are countless angels in heaven who perform their duties according to God's command. Among them are angels who watch, record, and report to God every deed of each person whether or not the person is a believer. On the Judgment Day, God remembers even a single word uttered by each individual, and rewards according to what he or she has done.

Likewise, all angels are spirits over whom God has control, and it is obvious that they protect and look after God's children even in heaven. Of course, there will not be any accidents or hazards in heaven since there is no darkness belonging to the enemy devil, but it is the natural duty for them to serve their masters. This duty is not forced by anybody but is carried out voluntarily according to the order and harmony of the spiritual realm; it is the natural duty assigned to angels.

To maintain the peaceful order of New Jerusalem

What, then, is the third reason that twelve angels guard the gates of New Jerusalem?

Heaven is a perfect spiritual realm without any flaw, and is run in perfect order. There is no hatred, quarrels, or commands but is operated and maintained only by God's orders.

A house divided against itself will fall. In the same way, even the world of Satan does not stand against itself but works according to a certain order (Mark 3:22-26). How much more justly, then, will the kingdom of God be established and operated in order?

For example, banquets held in New Jerusalem proceed according to the order. The saved souls in the Third, Second, and First Kingdoms and Paradise are to enter New Jerusalem on an invitation-only basis, again according to the spiritual order. There, they will please God and share the joy along with the residents of New Jerusalem.

If the saved souls in Paradise, the First, Second, and Third Kingdoms could freely enter New Jerusalem whenever they want, what would happen? Just as the value of even the best and most precious objects diminishes without being managed properly with the passage of time and usage, if the order in New Jerusalem were broken, its beauty could not be properly kept.

Therefore, for the peaceful order of New Jerusalem, there is a need for the twelve gates and the angels who guard each gate.

Of course, those believers in the Third Kingdom of Heaven and below cannot enter New Jerusalem freely even if there is no angel to guard the gate because of the difference in glory. Angels make sure the order is maintained more properly.

Names of the Twelve Tribes of Israel Inscribed on the Twelve Gates

What, then, is the reason for writing the names of the twelve tribes of Israel on the gates of New Jerusalem? The names of the twelve tribes of Israel symbolize the fact that the twelve gates of New Jerusalem began with the twelve tribes of Israel.

The background for making twelve gates

Adam and Eve, who were driven out from the Garden of Eden because of their sin of disobedience about 6,000 years ago, gave birth to many children while living on this earth. When the world was full of sins, every one except for Noah and his family, a righteous man among the people of his time, was punished and perished by water.

Then about 4,000 years ago Abraham was born, and when the time came, God established him as the forefather of faith and blessed him abundantly. God promised Abraham in Genesis 22:17-18.

Indeed I will greatly bless you, and I will greatly multiply your seed as the stars of the heavens and as the sand which is on the seashore; and your seed shall possess the gate of their enemies. In your seed all the

*nations of the earth shall be blessed, because you have
obeyed My voice.*

The faithful God established Jacob, grandson of Abraham, as
the founder of Israel, and made the foundation to form a nation
with his twelve sons. Then about 2,000 years ago, God sent Jesus
as a descendant from the tribe of Judah and opened the way of
salvation for all mankind.

In this way, God formed the people of Israel with twelve
tribes to fulfill the blessing that He had given to Abraham.
Furthermore, to symbolize and mark this fact, God made twelve
gates in New Jerusalem and inscribed the names of these twelve
tribes of Israel.

Now, let us take a closer look at Jacob, the forefather of Israel,
and the twelve tribes.

Jacob the forefather of Israel and his twelve sons

Jacob, grandson of Abraham and son of Isaac, took the
birthright from his elder brother Esau in a cunning way and had
to run away from his brother to his uncle Laban's. During his
twenty-year stay at Laban's house, God refined Jacob until he
became the forefather of Israel.

Genesis 29:21 onward explain in detail Jacob's marriages and
the birth of his twelve sons. Jacob loved Rachel and promised
to serve Laban seven years so that he could marry her, but he
was deceived by his uncle and came to marry Leah, her sister.
He had to promise Laban to serve another seven years to marry
her. Jacob finally married Rachel and loved Rachel more than he
loved Leah.

God had mercy on Leah, who was not loved by her husband,

and opened her womb. Leah gave birth to Reuben, Simeon, Levi, and Judah. Rachel was loved by Jacob, but could not give birth to sons for some time. She became jealous of her sister Leah and gave her maidservant Bilhah to her husband as a wife. Bilhah gave birth to Dan and Naphtali. When Leah could no longer conceive, she gave Jacob her maidservant Zilpah as a wife, and Zilpah gave birth to Gad and Asher.

Later, Leah received the agreement from Rachel on sleeping with Jacob in exchange for the first son Reuben's mandrakes. She gave birth to Issachar and Zebulun, and a daughter Dinah. Then, God remembered Rachel who was barren and opened her womb, and at this time she gave birth to Joseph. After the birth of Joseph, Jacob received a command from God to cross the Jabbok River and go back to his hometown with his two wives, two maidservants, and eleven sons.

Jacob went through trials at his uncle Laban's house for two decades. After that he humbled himself and prayed until his hip was wrenched at the Jabbok River, on the way to his hometown. He then received the new name "Israel" (Genesis 32:28). Israel also reconciled with his brother Esau and lived in the land of Canaan. He received the blessing of becoming the forefather of Israel and got the last of his sons, Benjamin, through Rachel.

The twelve tribes of Israel, chosen people of God

Joseph, who was loved the most by his father among Israel's twelve sons, was sold to Egypt at the age of seventeen by his brothers engulfed in jealousy. Within God's providence, however, at the age of thirty Joseph became the prime minister of Egypt. Knowing that there would be a severe famine in the land of Canaan, God had sent Joseph to Egypt first, and then allowed his whole family to move there so that they would increase in number large enough to form a nation.

In Genesis 49:3-28, Israel blesses his twelve sons just before he breathes his last, and they are the twelve tribes of Israel:

> *"Reuben, you are my firstborn;*
> *My might and the beginning of my strength (v. 3)...*
> *Simeon and Levi are brothers;*
> *Their swords are implements of violence (v. 5)...*
> *Judah, your brothers shall praise you (v. 8)...*
> *Zebulun will dwell at the seashore (v. 13)...*
> *Issachar is a strong donkey,*
> *Lying down between the sheepfolds (v. 14)...*
> *Dan shall judge his people,*
> *As one of the tribes of Israel (v. 16)...*
> *As for Gad, raiders shall raid him,*
> *But he will raid at their heels (v. 19)...*
> *As for Asher, his food shall be rich (v. 20)...*
> *Naphtali is a doe let loose,*
> *He gives beautiful words (v. 21)...*
> *Joseph is a fruitful bough,*
> *A fruitful bough by a spring (v. 22)...*
> *Benjamin is a ravenous wolf (v. 27)..."*

All these are the twelve tribes of Israel, and this is what their father said to them when he blessed them, giving each the blessing appropriate to him. The blessings were different because each son (tribe) was different in its characteristic, personality, deed, and nature.

Through Moses, God gave the Law to the twelve tribes of Israel who came out of Egypt, and began to lead them to the land of Canaan, flowing with milk and honey. In Deuteronomy 33:5-25, we see Moses blessing the people of Israel before his death.

> *"May Reuben live and not die,*
> *Nor his men be few (v. 6) ...*
> *Hear, O LORD, the voice of Judah,*
> *And bring him to his people (v. 7) ...*
> *Of Levi he said,*
> *"Let Your Thummim and Your Urim*
> *belong to Your godly man" (v. 8) ...*
> *Of Benjamin he said,*
> *"May the beloved of the LORD*
> *dwell in security by Him" (v. 9) ...*
> *Of Joseph he said,*
> *"Blessed of the LORD be his land,*
> *With the choice things of heaven, with the dew,*
> *And from the deep lying beneath" (v. 13) ...*
> *And those are the ten thousands of Ephraim,*
> *And those are the thousands of Manasseh (v. 17) ...*
> *Of Zebulun he said,*
> *"Rejoice, Zebulun, in your going forth,*
> *And, Issachar, in your tents" (v. 18) ...*
> *Of Gad he said,*
> *"Blessed is the one*
> *who enlarges Gad" (v. 20) ...*
> *Of Dan he said,*
> *"Dan is a lion's whelp,*
> *That leaps forth from Bashan" (v. 22) ...*
> *Of Naphtali he said,*
> *"O Naphtali, satisfied with favor,*
> *And full of the blessing of the LORD" (v. 23) ...*

More blessed than sons is Asher;
May he be favored by his brothers (v. 24) ... "

Levi, among Israel's twelve sons, was excluded from the twelve tribes in order to become priests and belong to God. Instead, Joseph's two sons Manasseh and Ephraim formed two tribes to replace the Levites.

Names of the twelve tribes inscribed on the twelve gates

Then, how can we, who are neither members of the twelve tribes of Israel nor direct descendants of Abraham, be saved and pass through the twelve gates on which the names of the twelve tribes are written?

We can find the answer to that question in the Book of Revelation 7:5-8:

And I heard the number of those who were sealed, one hundred and forty-four thousand sealed from every tribe of the sons of Israel: the tribe of Judah, twelve thousand were sealed, from the tribe of Reuben twelve thousand, from the tribe of Gad twelve thousand, the tribe of Asher twelve thousand, from the tribe of Naphtali twelve thousand, from the tribe of Manasseh twelve thousand, the tribe of Simeon twelve thousand, from the tribe of Levi twelve thousand, from the tribe of Issachar twelve thousand, the tribe of Zebulun twelve thousand, from the tribe of Joseph twelve thousand, from the tribe of Benjamin, twelve thousand were sealed.

In these verses, the name of the tribe of Judah comes first and the name of the tribe of Reuben follows it unlike in the Books of Genesis and Deuteronomy. And the name of the tribe of Dan is deleted and the name of the tribe of Manasseh is added.

It records the serious sin of the tribe of Dan in 1 Kings 12:28-31.

> *So the king consulted, and made two golden calves, and he said to them, "It is too much for you to go up to Jerusalem; behold your gods, O Israel, that brought you up from the land of Egypt." He set one in Bethel, and the other he put in Dan. Now this thing became a sin, for the people went to worship before the one as far as Dan. And he made houses on high places, and made priests from among all the people who were not of the sons of Levi.*

Jeroboam, who became the first king of the Northern Kingdom Israel, thought to himself that if the people went up to offer sacrifices at the temple of the LORD in Jerusalem, they would again give their allegiance to their lord, Rehoboam king of Judah. The king made two golden calves, and he set up one in Bethel, and the other in Dan. He prohibited the people from going up to Jerusalem to give sacrifices to God and enticed them to serve at Bethel and Dan.

The tribe of Dan committed the sin of idol-worshipping and made common people priests of God although none but the tribe of Levites could become priests. And they instituted a festival on the fifteenth day of the eighth month, like the festival held in Judah. All these sins were not able to be forgiven by God and they were forsaken by Him.

So, the name of the tribe of Dan was left out replaced by the name of the tribe of Manasseh. The fact that the name of the tribe of Manasseh was added was prophesied in Genesis 48:5. Jacob said to his son Joseph:

Now your two sons, who were born to you in the land of Egypt before I came to you in Egypt, are mine; Ephraim and Manasseh shall be mine, as Reuben and Simeon are.

Jacob, the father of Israel, already sealed Manasseh and Ephraim as his. So, in the Book of Revelation of the New Testament, it is found that the name of the tribe of Manasseh is recorded instead of that of Dan.

The fact that the name of the tribe of Manasseh is recorded among the twelve tribes of Israel in this way although he was not one of twelve leaders of Israel indicates that the Gentiles would take the place of the Israelites and be saved.

God laid the foundation of a nation through the twelve tribes of Israel. About two thousand years ago, He opened the gate of washing our sins through the precious blood Jesus Christ shed on the cross and allowed everyone to receive salvation with faith.

God chose the people of Israel who came out from the twelve tribes and called them "My people," but since they ultimately fell short of following God's will, the gospel went over to the Gentiles.

The Gentiles, the wild olive shoot that was grafted, have replaced God's chosen people of Israel that is olive shoot. That is why the apostle Paul said in Romans 2:28-29 that *"For he is not a Jew who is one outwardly, nor is circumcision that which is outward in the flesh. But he is a Jew who is one inwardly; and circumcision is that which is of the heart, by the Spirit, not by the letter; and his praise is not from men, but from God."*

In brief, the Gentiles have come to replace the people of Israel in accomplishing the providence of God just as the tribe of Dan was deleted and the tribe of Manasseh added. Therefore, even the Gentiles can enter New Jerusalem through the twelve gates so long as they possess the proper qualifications of faith.

Therefore, not only those who belong to twelve tribes of Israel, but also those who become descendants of Abraham in faith will receive salvation. When the Gentiles come into faith, God no longer considers them "the Gentiles" but instead as members of the twelve tribes. All nations will be saved through the twelve gates, and this is the righteousness of God.

After all, the "twelve tribes" of Israel spiritually refers to all God's children who are saved by faith, and God has written the names of the twelve tribes on the twelve gates of New Jerusalem to symbolize this fact.

However, as different countries and areas have different characteristics, the glory of each tribe of the twelve tribes and the twelve gates also varies in heaven.

Names of the Twelve Apostles Inscribed on the Twelve Foundations

What, then, is the reason the names of the twelve apostles are written on the twelve foundations of New Jerusalem?

To construct a building, there must be foundations to lay the pillars on. It is easy to estimate the size of the construction if you look at the depth of the dig. Foundations are very important because they have to support the weight of the entire structure.

In the same way, the twelve foundations were laid to put up the walls of New Jerusalem and twelve pillars, between which twelve gates were made. Then the twelve gates were made. The size of the twelve foundations and the twelve pillars is so enormous beyond our understanding, and we are going to delve into it in the next chapter.

Twelve foundations, more important than the twelve gates

Every shadow has the essence it casts. By the same token, the Old Testament is the shadow of the New Testament because the Old Testament testified to Jesus who was to come to this world as the Savior, and the New Testament records the ministry of Jesus who came to this world, fulfilled all prophecies, and accomplished the way of salvation (Hebrews 10:1).

God, who laid the foundation of a nation through the twelve tribes of Israel and proclaimed the Law through Moses, taught the twelve apostles through Jesus who fulfilled the Law with love and made them witnesses of the Lord to the ends of the earth. In this way, the twelve apostles are the heroes who made it possible to fulfill the Law of the Old Testament and build the City of New Jerusalem, acting not as a shadow but as the essence.

Therefore, the twelve foundations of New Jerusalem are more important than the twelve gates, and the role of the twelve apostles is more important than that of the twelve tribes.

Jesus and His twelve disciples

Jesus the Son of God, who came to this world in flesh, began His ministry at the age of thirty, called His disciples, and taught them. When the time came, Jesus empowered His apostles to drive out demons and heal the sick. Matthew 10:2-4 mentions the twelve apostles:

Now the names of the twelve apostles are these: The first, Simon, who is called Peter, and Andrew his brother; and James the son of Zebedee, and John his brother; Philip and Bartholomew; Thomas and Matthew the tax collector; James the son of Alphaeus, and Thaddaeus; Simon the Zealot, and Judas Iscariot, the one who betrayed Him.

As Jesus requested, they preached the gospel and performed the works of God's power. They testified to the living God and led many souls to the way of salvation. All of them except Judas Iscariot, who was instigated by Satan and ended up selling Jesus, witnessed the Lord's resurrection and ascension, and experienced the Holy Spirit through fervent prayers.

Then, as the Lord commissioned them, they received the Holy Spirit and the power and became the witnesses of the Lord in Jerusalem, all Judea and Samaria, and to the ends of the earth.

Matthias replaced Judas Iscariot

Acts 1:15-26 describes the process of replacing Judas Iscariot among the twelve apostles. They prayed to God and cast lots. This was done because the apostles wanted it to be done according to God's will, without intervention of any human thoughts. They finally selected an individual among the ones who had been taught by Jesus, a man named Matthias.

The reason Jesus still selected Judas Iscariot knowing that he would eventually betray lies here. The fact that Matthias was newly selected means that even the Gentiles could receive salvation. It also means the chosen servants of God today belong to the place of Matthias. Since the resurrection and the ascension of the Lord, there have been many servants of God who were selected by God Himself, and anybody who becomes one with the Lord can be selected as one of the Lord's apostles, the way Matthias became His apostle.

The servants of God selected by God Himself obey the will of their Master only with "Yes." If servants of God do not obey His will, they can and should not be called "servants of God" or "God's selected servants."

The twelve apostles including Matthias resembled the Lord, accomplished the holiness, obeyed the Lord's teachings and wholly fulfilled the will of God. They became the foundations of the world mission by fulfilling their duties until they became martyrs.

Names of the twelve apostles

Those who have been saved by faith, though they were neither sanctified nor faithful in all God's house, can visit New Jerusalem with an invitation, but they cannot dwell there forever. Thus, the reason the names of the twelve apostles are written on the twelve foundations is to remind us that only those who were sanctified and faithful in all God's house in this life can come into New Jerusalem.

The twelve tribes of Israel refer to all God's children who are saved by faith. Those who are sanctified and faithful with all their lives will have the qualifications to enter New Jerusalem. For these reasons, the twelve foundations are more important, and that is why the names of the twelve apostles are not written on the twelve gates but on the twelve foundations.

Why, then, did Jesus choose only twelve apostles? In His

perfect wisdom, God fulfills His providence which He designed before time began and accomplishes everything accordingly. Thus, we know that Jesus' selecting only twelve apostles was also carried out according to God's plan.

God, who formed twelve tribes in the Old Testament, selected twelve apostles, using the number 12 that stands for "light" and "perfection" in the New Testament as well, and the shadow of the Old Testament and the essence of the New Testament became a pair.

God does not change His mind and plan which He once designed, and keeps His Word. Therefore, we must believe all of the Word of God in the Bible, prepare ourselves as the Lord's brides to receive Him, and achieve and obtain qualifications necessary to enter New Jerusalem like the twelve apostles.

Jesus told us in Revelation 22:12, *"Behold, I am coming quickly, and My reward is with Me, to render to every man according to what he has done."*

What kind of Christian life should you lead if you truly believe that the Lord is coming back soon? You should not only be satisfied with having received salvation by faith in Jesus Christ, but must also try to cast your sins away and be faithful in all your duties.

I pray in the name of the Lord Jesus Christ that you will have the eternal glory and blessings in New Jerusalem like the forefathers of faith whose names are inscribed on the twelve gates and the twelve foundations!

Chapter 3

The Size of New Jerusalem

"The one who spoke with me had a gold measuring rod
to measure the city, and its gates and its wall.
The city is laid out as a square,
and its length is as great as the width;
and he measured the city with the rod,
fifteen hundred miles; its length
and width and height are equal.
And he measured its wall, seventy-two yards,
according to human measurements,
which are also angelic measurements."
- Revelation 21:15-17

Some believers think everybody who is saved will enter New Jerusalem which houses God's throne, or misunderstand that New Jerusalem is the heaven in its entirety. Yet, New Jerusalem is not the whole heaven, but only a part of the endless heaven. Only God's true children who are holy and sanctified can enter it. How vast, you may wonder, is the size of New Jerusalem, which God has prepared for His true children?

Let us delve into the size and shape of New Jerusalem, and the spiritual meanings hidden in them.

Measured by Golden Reed

It is natural for those with true faith and fervent hope for New Jerusalem to wonder about the shape and size of the City. Since it is the place for God's children who are sanctified and wholly resemble the Lord, God has prepared New Jerusalem so beautifully and magnificently.

In Revelation 21:15, you can read about an angel standing with golden reed to measure the size of the gates and walls of New Jerusalem. What, then, is the reason God made New Jerusalem be measured by golden reed?

The golden reed is a kind of straight edge used to measure distance in heaven. If you know the meaning of gold and reed, you can understand the reason God measures dimensions of New Jerusalem with the golden reed.

Gold stands for "faith" because it never changes over time. The gold of the golden reed symbolizes the fact that God's measurement is accurate and never changes, and all His promises will be kept.

Characteristics of reed that measures faith

Reed is tall and its edge is soft. It sways easily by the wind but never snaps; it possesses both softness and strength at the same time. Reed has gnarls, and this means that God rewards according to what one has done.

Thus, the reason God measures the City of New Jerusalem with the golden reed is to measure each one's faith accurately and return according to what he or she has done.

Now, let us consider the characteristics and spiritual meaning of reed to understand why God measures the dimensions of New Jerusalem with the golden reed.

First of all, reeds have very deep, strong roots. They are 1-3 meters, about 3-10 feet, tall, and live in stock in the sands of swamps or lakes. They may appear to have weak roots, but we cannot pull them out easily.

In the same way, God's children should also be firmly rooted in faith and stand on the rock of truth. Only when you have an unchanging faith that will not be shaken under any circumstances, will you be able to enter New Jerusalem whose dimensions are measured by the golden reed. It is for this reason that the apostle Paul prayed for the believers of Ephesus, *"so that Christ may dwell in your hearts through faith; and that you, being rooted and grounded in love"* (Ephesians 3:17).

Second, reeds have very soft edges. Since Jesus had a soft and meek heart, remindful of reeds, He never quarreled or cried out. Even when others criticized or persecuted Him, Jesus would not debate but instead went away.

Therefore, those who hope for New Jerusalem should have meek hearts like that of Jesus. If you feel uncomfortable when others point out your mistakes or admonish you, it means you still have a hard and proud heart. If you have a soft and meek heart like fluff, you can accept those things with gladness without any feeling of regret or dissatisfaction.

Third, reeds sway easily by the winds but do not break easily. After a strong typhoon, big trees sometimes get uprooted, but reeds do not usually break even by the strong winds because they are soft. People of this world sometimes compare the minds and hearts of women with reeds to express it in a bad way, but God's comparison is the opposite. Reeds are soft and may appear very weak, yet they have the strength not to snap even in strong winds, and they have the beauty of their elegant, white flowers.

Because reeds have all aspects of things such as softness, strength, and beauty, they can symbolize the justice of certain judgments. Such characteristics of reeds can also be attributed to the state of Israel as well. Israel has a relatively small territory and population, and is surrounded by hostile neighbors. Israel may look like a weak country, but it never "snaps" under any circumstances. This is because they have such strong faith in God, faith that is rooted in the forefathers of faith including Abraham. Although they look like they will physically crumble in an instant, the Israelites' faith in God allows them to stand firm.

By the same token, in order to enter New Jerusalem, we must have the faith that never falters under any circumstances, taking the root in Jesus Christ who is the rock, like reeds with strong roots.

Fourth, the stems of reeds are straight and smooth so that they have been often used to make roofs, arrows, or nibs on pens. The straight stem also implies moving forward. Faith is said to be "alive" only when it keeps on advancing. Those who improve and develop themselves will grow in their faith day by day, and keep on advancing towards heaven.

God selects these good vessels who advance towards heaven, refines and makes them perfect so that these people will be able to enter New Jerusalem. Therefore, we should advance towards heaven like the leaves that sprout from the end of a straight stem.

Fifth, as many poets wrote about flowers of reed to depict peaceful scenery, the appearance of reeds is very soft and beautiful, and their leaves are graceful and elegant. As 2 Corinthians 2:15 says, *"For we are a fragrance of Christ to*

God among those who are being saved and among those who are perishing," those standing on the rock of faith give out the aroma of Christ. Those who have this kind of hearts have graceful and comforting faces, and people can experience heaven through them. Therefore, in order to enter New Jerusalem, we have to give out the beautiful aroma of Christ that is like the soft flowers and elegant leaves of reeds.

Sixth, the leaves of reeds are thin and the edges are sharp enough to cut the skin just by grazing. In the same way, those who have faith must not compromise with sins but become like blades by casting away the evil.

Daniel, who was a minister of the great Persia and was loved by the king, faced a trial in which he was sentenced to be put into the lion's den by evil men who were jealous of him. Yet, he did not compromise at all, but held fast to his faith. As a result, God sent His angel to close the mouths of the lions, and allowed Daniel to glorify God greatly in front of the king and all the people.

God is pleased with the kind of faith Daniel had, the kind that does not compromise with the world. He protects those who have this kind of faith from all kinds of hardships and tests, and allows them to glorify Him in the end. Also, He blesses and makes them "the head, not the tail" wherever they go (Deuteronomy 28:1-14).

Moreover, as Proverbs 8:13 tells us, *"The fear of the LORD is to hate evil,"* if you have evil in your heart, you have to cast it away through fervent prayers and fasting. Only when you do not compromise with sins but hate the evil, will you be sanctified and have the qualifications to enter New Jerusalem.

We have considered the reason God measures the City of New Jerusalem with the golden reeds by looking at the six characteristics of the reeds. The use of golden reed allows us to know that God measures our faith accurately and rewards us exactly as we have done in this life, and that He fulfills His promises.

A Cube-shaped New Jerusalem

God has specifically recorded the size and the shape of New Jerusalem in the Bible. Revelation 21:16 tells us that the City has a cubic shape with fifteen hundred miles (12,000 stadia or 2,400 km) in length, width, and height. At this some may wonder, 'Won't we feel like we are locked in?' Yet, God has made the interior of New Jerusalem so comfortable and pleasant. Also, one cannot see through the City of New Jerusalem from outside, but people inside the walls can see the outside. In other words, there is no reason to feel uncomfortable or confined inside the walls.

The same in width, length, and height

What, then, is the reason God has made New Jerusalem in a cubic shape? The same lengths and widths represent order, accuracy, justice, and righteousness of the City of New Jerusalem. God is controlling all things in order so that countless stars, the moon, the sun, the solar system, and the rest of the universe are moving precisely and accurately without any glitch. Likewise, God has made the City of New Jerusalem in a square shape to express that He controls all things and the history in order, and fulfills everything until the end with precision.

New Jerusalem has equal widths and lengths, and twelve gates and twelve foundations, three on each side. This symbolizes that no matter where one lives on this earth, the rules will be applied fairly to those who have the qualifications to enter New Jerusalem. Namely, people who are qualified by the measurement of the golden reed will enter New Jerusalem regardless of their sex, age, or race.

This is because God, with His straight and just character, judges with justice and measures the qualifications to enter New Jerusalem accurately. Furthermore, a square represents north, south, east, and west. God has made New Jerusalem, and calls His perfect children who are saved with faith among all nations from all four directions.

Revelation 21:16 reads, *"The city is laid out as a square, and its length is as great as the width; and he measured the city with the rod, fifteen hundred miles; its length and width and height are equal."* 'Fifteen hundred miles' is converted into 'Twelve thousand (12,000) stadia' with a Greek distance-measuring unit, when it is converted once again to roughly 2,400 kilometers. Thus, the cubic-shaped New Jerusalem measures 2,400 km in width, length, and height.

Also, Revelation 21:17 reads, *"And he measured its wall, seventy-two yards, according to human measurements, which are also angelic measurements."*

The walls of the City of New Jerusalem are seventy-two yards thick. 'Seventy-two yards' is converted into about '144 cubits' or 65 meters, or 213 feet. As the City of New Jerusalem is enormous, its walls are also incomparably thick.

Chapter 4

Made of Pure Gold
and Jewels of All Colors

"The material of the wall was jasper;
and the city was pure gold, like clear glass."

- Revelation 21:18

Suppose you had all the wealth and authority to build a house in which you and your loved one were to live for eternity. How would you like to design it? What materials would you use? No matter what the cost, the length of time, and the amount of manpower may be required to build it, you would probably want to build it in the most beautiful and charming way.

By the same token, would our Father God not have wanted to build and adorn New Jerusalem beautifully with the best materials of heaven to stay there with His lovely children forever? Moreover, each material in New Jerusalem has a different meaning to recognize the times we have endured with faith and love on this earth, and everything there is magnificent.

It is only natural for those who long for New Jerusalem in their deep hearts to want to know more about New Jerusalem.

God knows the hearts of these people and has given us various pieces of information on New Jerusalem, including its size, shape, and even the thickness of the wall, in detail in the Bible.

Of what, then, is the City of New Jerusalem made?

Adorned With Pure Gold
and All Kinds of Jewels

New Jerusalem, which God has prepared for His children, is made of pure gold that never changes and decorated with other jewels. In heaven there is no material, like soil on this earth, which changes with the passing of time. The roads in New Jerusalem are made of pure gold and the foundations made with jewels. If the sands on the shore of the river of the water of life are gold and silver, how much more stunning would the materials be for other buildings?

New Jerusalem: God's masterpiece

Among all world-famous buildings, their glitter, value, elegance, and delicacy all differ from one structure to another depending on the materials used to build them. Marbles are much shinier, more elegant and beautiful than sand, wood, or cement.

Can you imagine how beautiful and gorgeous would it be if you built an entire building with expensive gold and jewels? Moreover, how much more beautiful and fantastic the buildings in heaven made of the most beautiful materials would be!

The gold and jewels in heaven made by God's power are much different in their quality, color, and the refinement from the ones on this earth. Their purity and the light that shines so beautifully cannot be sufficiently expressed with words.

Even on this earth, many kinds of vessels can be made from

the same clay. They can be expensive china or cheap clayware depending on the kind of clay and the level of skills of the potter. It took thousands of years for God to build New Jerusalem, His masterpiece, which is filled with the magnificent, precious, and perfect glory of the City's Architect.

Pure gold stands for faith and eternal life

Pure gold is a hundred percent gold without any impurities, and is the only thing that never changes on this earth. Due to this trait, many countries used it as the standard for their currencies and exchange rates, and it is used for decorations and industrial purposes as well. Pure gold is sought and loved by many people.

The reason God gave us gold on this earth is to allow us to realize that there are things that never change, and that an eternal world does exist. Things on this earth get worn out and change as time passes. If we had only such things, it would be hard for us to realize that there is an eternal heaven with our limited knowledge.

This is why God permits us to know that there are eternal things through this gold that never changes. It is for us to realize that there is something that never changes and to have hope for the eternal heaven. Pure gold stands for the spiritual faith that never changes. Therefore, if you are wise, you will try to gain faith that is like the never-changing pure gold.

There are many things made of pure gold in heaven. Imagine how thankful we would be to just look at the heaven made of pure gold, which we have considered the most precious in this life on this earth!

Yet, those who are unwise cherish gold only as a means to increase or display their wealth. Accordingly, they stay away from

God and do not love Him, and they will eventually fall into the lake of fire or burning sulfur in hell, and perpetually regret, saying, "I wouldn't be suffering in hell only if I considered faith as precious as I considered gold so precious."

Therefore, I hope you will be wise and possess heaven by trying to obtain the unchanging faith, not the gold of this world that you will have to leave once your life on this earth will have come to an end.

Jewels stand for God's glory and love

Jewels are solid and have high index of refraction. They have and give out beautiful colors and lights. Since not much of them is produced, they are loved by many people and considered precious. In heaven, God will clothe those who possess heaven with faith with fine linen and decorate them with many jewels to express His love.

People love jewels and try to make themselves look more beautiful by decorating with various adornments. How delightful would it be when God gives you many brilliant jewels in heaven?

One may ask, "Why do we need jewels in heaven?" Jewels in heaven represent God's glory, and the amount of jewels one is rewarded represents the extent of God's love for that person.

There are countless sorts and colors of jewels in heaven. For the twelve foundations of New Jerusalem, there are sapphire of a transparent dark blue color; emerald of transparent green; ruby of dark red; and chrysolite of transparent yellowish green. Beryl is of bluish green that reminds us of clear sea water, and topaz has a mild orange color. Chrysoprase is of semi-transparent dark green, and amethyst has a light violet or dark purple color.

Other than these, there are innumerable jewels that have and give out beautiful colors such as jasper, chalcedony, sardonyx, and jacinth. All these jewels have different names and significance just as jewels on this earth do. The colors and the names of each jewel are combined to show the dignity, pride, value and the glory.

Just as jewels on this earth give out different colors and lights at different angles, jewels in heaven have various lights and colors, and the jewels in New Jerusalem especially shine and reflect twofold or threefold lights.

Quite obviously, those jewels are more beautiful beyond comparison than the ones found on this earth because God Himself polished the ores with the power of creation. That is why the apostle John said the beauty of New Jerusalem is like the most precious stones.

Also, the jewels in New Jerusalem give out much more beautiful lights than those of other dwelling places because God's children who enter New Jerusalem will have completely accomplished God's heart and given glory to Him. Thus, both the inside and outside of New Jerusalem are adorned with many kinds of beautiful jewels of various colors. Yet, these jewels are not given to everybody, but rewarded according to each one's deeds of faith on this earth.

The Walls of New Jerusalem Made of Jasper

Revelation 21:18 tells us that the walls of New Jerusalem were "made of jasper." Can you imagine how grand the walls of New Jerusalem made with jasper all around would be?

Jasper stands for spiritual faith

Jasper found on this earth is usually a solid and opaque stone. Its colors vary, ranging from green, red, to yellowish green. Some of its colors are mixed or some of it have spots. Depending on the color, the solidity differs. Jasper is relatively cheap and some of them easily break, but heavenly jasper made by God never changes or breaks. Heavenly jasper has a bluish white color and is transparent so that it feels like you are looking into a body of clear water. Although it cannot be compared to anything on this earth, it is similar to brilliant, bluish sun lights reflected against waves in the ocean.

This jasper stands for spiritual faith. Faith is the most essential and fundamental element in leading a Christian life. Without faith you can neither receive salvation nor please God. Furthermore, without the kind of faith that can please God, you cannot enter New Jerusalem.

Therefore, the City of New Jerusalem is built with faith, and the jewel that can express the color of this faith is jasper. That is why the walls of New Jerusalem are made of jasper.

If the Bible tells us "The walls of New Jerusalem are made with faith," would people be able to understand such an expression? Of course it could not be understood with human thoughts and it would be very hard for people to even try to imagine how beautifully New Jerusalem is decorated.

The walls made of jasper shine clearly with the light of God's glory and are decorated with many patterns and designs.

The City of New Jerusalem is the masterpiece of God the Creator and the place of eternal rest for the best fruit from the 6,000 years of the human cultivation. How magnificent, beautiful, and brilliant would the City be?

We must realize that New Jerusalem is made with the best technology and equipment whose mechanics we cannot even fathom.

Although the walls are transparent, the inside is not visible from the outside. However, this does not mean that people inside the City will feel like they are confined inside the city walls. New Jerusalem residents can see outside the City from within and this feels as if there were no walls. How wondrous it would be!

Made of Pure Gold Like Clear Glass

The latter part of Revelation 21:18 reads, *"The city was pure gold, like clear glass."* Let us now consider the characteristics of gold to help ourselves imagine New Jerusalem and grasp its beauty.

Pure gold has an unchanging value

Gold does not get oxidized in the air or water. It does not change over time and displays no chemical reaction by other substances. Gold always keeps the same, beautiful brilliance. Gold on this earth is too soft, so we make an alloy; in heaven, gold is not too soft. Also, gold or other jewels in heaven give out different colors and have different solidity than the ones found on the earth, because they receive the light of God's glory.

Even on this earth, the elegance and value of jewels differ according to the skills and techniques of the craftsman. How precious and beautiful would the jewels of New Jerusalem be since they are touched and carved by God Himself?

There is no greed or desire for beautiful and good objects in heaven. On the earth people tend to love jewels for their lavishness and vacant fame, but in heaven they love jewels spiritually because they know the spiritual significance of each and they apprehend the love of God who prepared and decorated heaven with beautiful jewels.

God made New Jerusalem with pure gold

Why, then, has God made the City of New Jerusalem with pure gold that is as clear as glass? As explained before, pure gold spiritually stands for faith, hope that is born by faith, riches, honors, and authority. "Hope born by faith" means you can receive salvation, hope for New Jerusalem, cast your sins away, endeavor to sanctify yourself, and look forward to the rewards with hope because you have faith.

Therefore, God has made this City with pure gold so that those who enter it with passionate hope would forever be filled with gratitude and happiness.

Revelation 21:18 tells us that New Jerusalem is "like clear glass." This is to express how clear and fine the scenery of New Jerusalem is. The gold in heaven is clear and pure as glass unlike opaque gold found on this earth.

New Jerusalem is clear and fine and without any blemish because it is made of pure gold. That is why the apostle John observed the City to be like *"pure gold, like clear glass."*

Try to imagine the City of New Jerusalem made of pure, fine gold and many kinds of beautiful jewels with many colors.

After accepting the Lord, I considered gold or jewels like ordinary stones and never desired to possess them. I was full of hope for heaven, and did not love things of this world. Yet, when I prayed to learn about heaven, the Lord said to me, *"In heaven everything is made of beautiful jewels and gold; you should love these."* He did not mean that I should begin collecting gold and jewels. Instead, I was to realize God's providence and the spiritual significance of the jewels and love them the way God saw it fit.

I urge you to *spiritually love* gold and jewels. When you see gold, you can think, "I should have faith like pure gold." When you see other various jewels, you can hope for heaven, saying, "How beautiful will my house in heaven be?"

I pray in the name of the Lord Jesus Christ that you may possess a heavenly house made of never-changing gold and magnificent jewels by obtaining faith like pure gold and running towards heaven.

Chapter 5

The Significance
of the Twelve Foundations

*"The foundation stones of the city wall were adorned
with every kind of precious stone.
The first foundation stone was jasper; the second,
sapphire; the third, chalcedony; the fourth,
emerald; the fifth, sardonyx; the sixth,
sardius; the seventh, chrysolite; the eighth,
beryl; the ninth, topaz; the tenth,
chrysoprase; the eleventh,
jacinth; the twelfth, amethyst."*

- Revelation 21:19-20

The apostle John wrote about the twelve foundations in detail.
Why did John make such a thorough report of New Jerusalem?
God wants His children to possess eternal life and true faith by
knowing about the spiritual significances of the twelve foundations
of New Jerusalem.

Why, then, did God make the twelve foundations with twelve
precious stones? The combination of the twelve precious stones
represents the heart of Jesus Christ and God, the culmination
of love. Thus, if you understand the spiritual significance of
each of the twelve precious stones, you could easily distinguish

how much your heart resembles that of Jesus Christ, and how qualified you are to enter New Jerusalem.

Let us now examine the twelve precious stones and their spiritual significances.

Jasper: Spiritual Faith

Jasper, the first foundation of the walls of New Jerusalem, stands for spiritual faith. Faith can generally be divided into "spiritual faith" and "fleshly faith." While fleshly faith is the faith filled only with knowledge, spiritual faith is the faith accompanied by deed originating from the depths of one's heart. What God wants is not fleshly but spiritual faith. If you do not have spiritual faith, your "faith" will not be accompanied by deed, and you can neither please God nor enter New Jerusalem.

Spiritual faith is the basis of Christian life

"Spiritual faith" refers to the kind of faith with which one can believe all of the Word of God deep in his heart. If you have this sort of faith followed by deeds, you will try to be sanctified and run towards New Jerusalem. Spiritual faith is the most important element in leading a Christian life. Without faith, you cannot be saved, receive answer to your prayers, or have hope for heaven.

Hebrews 11:6 reminds us, *"And without faith it is impossible to please Him for he who comes to God must believe that He is and that He is a rewarder of those who seek Him."* If you have true faith, you will believe in God who rewards you, and then you can be faithful, fight against sins to cast them away and walk the narrow way. And you will be able to fervently do good and enter New Jerusalem following the Holy Spirit.

Thus, faith is the basis of a Christian life. Just as a building cannot be safe without firm foundation, you cannot lead a proper Christian life without firm faith. That is why Jude 1:20-21 urges us, *"But you, beloved, building yourselves up on your most holy faith, praying in the Holy Spirit, keep yourselves in the love of God, waiting anxiously for the mercy of our Lord Jesus Christ to eternal life."*

Abraham, the Father of Faith

The best biblical figure of believing the Word of God unchangingly and showing the deeds of obedience completely is Abraham. He was called 'the Father of Faith' because he showed perfect deeds of faith unchangingly.

He received a word of great blessing from God when he was 75. It was the promise that God would make a great nation through Abraham and Abraham would be the source of blessing. He believed this word and left his hometown, but he couldn't have a son who would become the heir for more than 20 years.

So much time passed that Abraham and his wife Sarah both became too old to have a child. Even in this kind of situation, Romans 4:19-20 says, *"He did not waver in unbelief."* He grew strong in faith, and believed the promise of God completely; so that he gained his son Isaac at the age of 100.

But there was one more occasion where Abraham's faith shed its light even more brightly. It was when God commanded Abraham to offer his only son, Isaac, as a sacrifice. Abraham did not doubt the Word of God saying that God would give him countless descendants through Isaac. Because he had firm faith in the Word of God, he thought God would revive Isaac, even if he offered him as a burnt sacrifice.

That is why he immediately obeyed the Word of God. Through this, Abraham was more than qualified to become the father of faith. Also, through Abraham's descendants, the nation of Israel was formed. It means the fruit of his faith was abundantly borne in the flesh as well.

Because he believed God and His Word, he obeyed it as he was told. This is an example of spiritual faith.

Peter received keys of the kingdom of heaven

Let us consider an individual who had this kind of spiritual faith. What kind of faith did the apostle Peter have, so that his name is inscribed on one of the foundations of New Jerusalem? Even before he was called as a disciple, we know Peter obeyed Jesus; for instance, when Jesus told him to let down the nets for a catch, he complied right away (Luke 5:3-6). Also, when Jesus told him to bring a donkey and her colt, he obeyed with faith (Matthew 21:1-7). Peter obeyed when Jesus told him to go to the lake, catch a fish, and get a coin from it (Matthew 17:27). Moreover, he walked on water like Jesus, although it was only for a moment. We can have some idea that Peter had an enormous faith.

As a result, Jesus deemed Peter's faith righteous and gave him keys of the kingdom of heaven so that whatever he bound on earth should have been bound in heaven, and whatever he loosed on earth should have been loosed in heaven (Matthew 16:19). Peter gained a more perfect faith after he received the Holy Spirit, boldly testified to Jesus Christ, and devoted himself for the kingdom of God for the rest of his life until he became a martyr.

We ought to advance towards heaven the way Peter did, give

glory to God, and possess New Jerusalem with the faith that can please Him.

Sapphire: Uprightness and Integrity

Sapphire, the second foundation of the walls of New Jerusalem, gives out a transparent, dark, blue color. What, then, does sapphire mean spiritually? It stands for uprightness and integrity of the truth itself, which stands firmly against any temptations or threats of this world. Sapphire is a stone that stands for the light of truth that can keep going straight without changing and the "upright heart" that deems all of God's will accurate.

Daniel and his three friends

A good example of the spiritual uprightness and integrity in the Bible is found in Daniel and his three friends—Shadrach, Meshach and Abed-nego. Daniel did not compromise with anything that was not in accordance with God's righteousness, even if that was an order from his king. Daniel held fast to his righteousness before God until he was put into the lion's den. God was so pleased with the integrity of Daniel's faith that He protected Daniel by sending His angel to close the mouths of the lions, and allowed him to greatly glorify God.

Daniel 3:16-18 reads that Daniel's three friends also clung to the faith with their upright hearts until they were thrown into the blazing furnace. In order not to commit the sin of worshipping idols, they boldly confessed before the king as follows:

O Nebuchadnezzar, we do not need to give you an

answer concerning this matter. If it be so, our God whom we serve is able to deliver us from the furnace of blazing fire; and He will deliver us out of your hand, O king. But even if He does not, let it be known to you, O king, that we are not going to serve your gods or worship the golden image that you have set up.

In the end, even though they had been put into the furnace seven times hotter than usual, Daniel's three friends were not scorched even a little because God was with them. How amazing it is that not even a hair of their head was singed and there was not a smell of fire on them! The king who witnessed all this gave glory to God, and promoted Daniel's three friends.

We should ask in faith, without any doubt

James 1:6-8 tells us how much God hates hearts that are not upright:

But he must ask in faith without any doubting, for the one who doubts is like the surf of the sea, driven and tossed by the wind. For that man ought not to expect that he will receive anything from the Lord, being a double-minded man, unstable in all his ways.

If we do not have upright hearts and doubt God even a little, we are double-minded. Those who doubt are prone to be easily shaken by temptations of this world because they are inattentive and sly. Moreover, those who are "double-minded" cannot see the glory of God because they are unable to either demonstrate their faith or obey. This is why we are reminded in James 1:7, *"that man ought not to expect that he will receive anything from the Lord."*

Soon after the founding of my church, my three daughters almost died from carbon monoxide poisoning. Yet, I did not worry at all and had no thought of taking them to a hospital because I completely believed in the almighty God. I simply went up to the altar and kneeled down to pray in thanksgiving. After that, I prayed in faith, "I command in the name of Jesus Christ! Poisonous gas, go away!" Then my daughters, who had been unconscious, stood up immediately one by one as I prayed for each one. A number of church members who witnessed this were so amazed and joyful, and greatly glorified God.

If we have faith that never compromises with this world and upright hearts that please God, we can boundlessly glorify Him and lead blessed lives in Christ.

Chalcedony: Innocence and Sacrificial Love

Chalcedony, the third foundation of the walls of New Jerusalem, spiritually symbolizes innocence and sacrificial love.

Innocence is the state of being clean and unsoiled in action and the heart that has no faults. When one is able to sacrifice himself with this purity of the heart, this is the heart of spirit contained in chalcedony.

Sacrificial love is a kind of love that never asks anything in return if it is for the righteousness and the kingdom of God. If one has sacrificial love, he will be satisfied only with the fact that he loves others in any kind of situations and not seek anything in return. This is because spiritual love does not seek one's own benefit but only the good of others.

With fleshly love, however, one will feel empty, saddened, and heartbroken if he is not loved back by others because this kind of love is in essence selfish. Therefore, one with fleshly love without a sacrificial heart can eventually hate others or become enemies with those with whom he used to be close.

Therefore, we are to realize that true love is the love of the Lord, who loved all mankind and became an atoning sacrifice.

Sacrificial love which seeks nothing in return

Our Lord Jesus, being in very nature God, made Himself nothing, and lowered Himself and came to the earth in flesh to save all mankind. He was born in a stable and laid in a manger to save the people who are like animals, and led a poor life all His life to save us from poverty. Jesus healed the sick, strengthened the weak, gave hope to the hopeless, and befriended the neglected. He showed us only goodness and love but for that He was mocked, whipped, and in the end crucified, wearing the crown of thorns on His head, by evil ones who did not realize He had come as our Savior.

Jesus, even as He was suffering from the pain of crucifixion, prayed to God the Father in love for those who mocked and crucified Him. He was blameless and spotless, but sacrificed Himself for human beings who are sinners. Our Lord gave this sacrificial love to all mankind and wants everyone to love one another. Thus, we, who have received this kind of love from the Lord, should not want or expect anything in return if we truly love others.

Ruth who showed sacrificial love

Ruth was not an Israelite, but a Moabite woman. She married a son of Naomi, who had come to the land of Moab to escape the famine in Israel. Naomi had two sons, and both of them married Moabite women. But both of her two sons died there.

Under these conditions, when Naomi heard the famine in Israel had been over, she wanted to go back to Israel. Naomi suggested to her daughters-in-law that they should stay in Moab, their homeland. One of them refused at first, but finally went back to her parents. But Ruth insisted that she follow her mother-in-law.

If Ruth had not had sacrificial love, she couldn't have done it. Ruth had to support her mother-in-law because she was very old. Furthermore, she was going to live in a land completely foreign to her. There was no reward for her, even though she served her mother-in-law very well.

Ruth showed the sacrificial love towards her mother-in-law with whom she had no blood-relation and thus who was like a complete stranger. It was because Ruth also believed in God whom her mother-in-law believed. It means Ruth's sacrificial love did not just come from her sense of duty. It was spiritual love that came out from faith in God.

Ruth came to Israel with her mother-in-law and worked very hard. In the daytime she gleaned in the fields to gain food and served her mother-in-law with it. This genuine deed of goodness naturally became well-known to the people there. Finally, Ruth received many blessings through Boaz, who was the kinsman-redeemer among the relatives of her mother-in-law.

Many people think that, if they humble and sacrifice themselves, their value will be lowered, too. That is why they cannot sacrifice or humble themselves. But those who sacrifice themselves without any selfish motives with a pure heart will be revealed before God and the people. The goodness and love will shine for others as spiritual lights. God likens the light of this sacrificial love to the light of chalcedony, the third foundation stone.

Emerald: Righteousness and Cleanliness

Emerald, the fourth foundation of the walls of New Jerusalem, is green and symbolizes the beauty and tender green of the nature. Emerald spiritually symbolizes righteousness and cleanliness and stands for the fruit of light as recorded in Ephesians 5:9 that reads, *"For the fruit of the Light consists in all goodness and righteousness and truth."* The color that has the harmony of 'all goodness and righteousness and truth' is the same as the spiritual light of emerald. Only when we have all of the goodness, righteousness and truth can we have true righteousness in the sight of God.

It cannot be only goodness without righteousness or just righteousness without goodness. And that goodness and righteousness have to be truthful. Truth is something that never changes. Therefore, even if we have goodness and righteousness, it is meaningless without truthfulness.

The "righteousness" God recognizes is casting away sins, wholly keeping the commands found in the Bible, cleansing oneself from all kinds of unrighteous matters, being faithful with all one's life, and the like. Also, seeking God's kingdom and righteousness after God's will, straight and disciplined actions, not going astray from justice, standing firmly for being in the right, and the rest all belong to "righteousness" recognized by God.

No matter how meek and good we may be, we will not bear the fruit of light unless we are righteous. Suppose somebody grabs your father by the throat and insults him although he is innocent. If you keep quiet and watch your father suffer, we cannot call it true righteousness; you could not be said to be doing your duty as a son towards your father.

Therefore, goodness without righteousness is not spiritual "goodness" in the sight of God. How can a sneaky and indecisive mind be good? Conversely, neither can righteousness without goodness be "righteousness" in God's sight but only in one's own sight.

Righteousness and cleanliness of David

David was the second king of Israel, just after Saul. When Saul was the king, Israel was fighting against Philistines. David pleased God with his faith and defeated Goliath. Through this, Israel won the victory.

And when people loved David after this, Saul tried to kill David out of his jealousy. Saul had already been forsaken by God because of his arrogance and disobedience. God promised that He would make David the king in the place of Saul.

In this situation, David treated Saul with goodness, righteousness, and truthfulness. Being innocent, David had to keep running from Saul who was trying to kill him for a long time. One time, David had a very good chance to kill Saul. The warriors who were with David were happy and wanted to kill Saul, but David stopped them from killing him.

1 Samuel 24:6 says, *"So [David] said to his men, 'Far be it from me because of the LORD that I should do this thing to my lord, the LORD's anointed, to stretch out my hand against him, since he is the LORD's anointed.'"*
Even though Saul was forsaken by God, David could not hurt Saul, who had been anointed as the king by God. Because the authority to let Saul live or die was with God, David did not go beyond his powers. God says this heart of David is righteous.

His righteousness was revealed along with touching goodness. Saul tried to kill him, but David spared Saul's life. This is such great goodness. He did not repay evil for evil, but only repaid it with good words and deeds. This goodness and righteousness was truthful, which means it came out from truthfulness itself.
When Saul knew that David spared his life, he was touched by that goodness and seemed to have a change of heart. But soon his thoughts changed again, and again he tried to kill David. Once again, David had a chance to kill Saul, but as before he let Saul live. David showed goodness and righteousness without change that could be acknowledged by God.

Then, if David had killed Saul at the first chance, could he have become the king sooner without going through so much suffering? Of course he could have. Even if we have to go through more sufferings and difficulties in reality, we should have the heart to choose the righteousness of God. And if we are once recognized by God to be righteous, the level of God's guaranteeing us will be different.

David did not kill Saul with his own hand. Saul was killed at the hands of Gentiles. And as God attested him, David became the king of Israel. Furthermore, after David became the king, he could make a very strong nation. The most fundamental reason is because God was very pleased with the just and pure heart of David.

By the same token, we have to be harmonious and perfect in goodness, righteousness, and truth so that we can bear the abundant fruit of the light—the fruit of emerald, the fourth foundation and give out the fragrance of righteousness with which God is pleased.

Sardonyx: Spiritual Faithfulness

Sardonyx, the fifth foundation of the walls of New Jerusalem, spiritually symbolizes faithfulness. If we just do what we are supposed to do, we cannot say we are faithful. We can say we are faithful when we do more than what we are supposed to do. To do more than what has been given as our duties we cannot be lazy. We have to be diligent and hardworking in all things in doing our duties and then we must do more than that.

Suppose you are an employee. Then, if you just do your work well, can we say you are faithful? You just did what you were supposed to do, so we cannot say you are hardworking and faithful. You should accomplish not just the work entrusted to you, but also try to do things that were not originally given to you with all your heart and mind. Only then can people say that you are faithful.

The kind of hardworking faithfulness recognized by God is

to do your duty with all your heart, mind, soul, and life. And this kind of faithfulness has to be actualized in all areas: church, workplace, and family. Then, we say you are faithful in all God's house.

To be spiritually faithful

To have spiritual faithfulness, we should first have a righteous heart. We should desire for the kingdom of God to be enlarged, for the church to have revival and growth, for the workplace to be prosperous, and for our families to be happy. If we do not just seek our own, but desire for others and the community to be prosperous, this is to have a righteous heart.

To be faithful, along with having this righteous heart, we should have a sacrificial heart. If we just think, "The most important thing is my prosperity, not whether or not the church is growing up," we will probably not sacrifice for the church. We cannot find faithfulness from this kind of person. Also, God cannot say this kind of heart is the heart that is righteous.

In addition to this righteousness, if we also have a heart of sacrifice, we will work faithfully for the salvation of souls and the church. Even if we don't have a special duty, we will preach the gospel diligently. Even if nobody asks us to do it, we will take care of other souls. We will also sacrifice our leisure time to take care of the souls. We will also spend our own money for the benefit of other souls and give them all our love and faithfulness.

In order to be faithful in all aspects, we should also have goodness of heart. Those who are good in heart will not incline toward just one side or the other. If we have neglected a certain point, we will not be comfortable about it if we have goodness in heart.

If you have goodness in heart, you will be faithful in all the duties that you have. You would not neglect the other group by thinking, "Since I am the leader of this group, the members of the other group will understand why I cannot attend that meeting." You can feel it within your goodness that you should not neglect the other group. So, even if you cannot be present in the meeting, you do something and care for the other group, too.

The magnitude of this kind of attitude will be different according to the magnitude of goodness you have. If you have little goodness, you will not even really care very much about the other group. But if you have a greater goodness, you will not just ignore it when something causes discomfort to your heart. You know what kind of acts are acts of goodness, and if you are not accomplishing that goodness, it is difficult for you to bear it. You will have peace only when you do in acts of goodness.

Those who are good in heart will soon have some discomfort in heart if they don't do what they are supposed to do in any given circumstances, whether in workplace or home. They don't even give excuses that the situation didn't allow it.

For example, suppose there is a female member who has many titles in the church. She spends a lot of time in the church. Relatively speaking then, she spends less time with her husband and children than she did previously.

If she is really good in heart and faithful in all aspects, as the amount of time has decreased, she has to give her husband and children more love and more care for them. She has to do her best in all aspects and in all kinds of works.

Then, people around her will be able to feel the truthful

aroma of her heart and be satisfied. Because they feel the goodness and truthful love, they will try to understand and help her. As a result, she will have peace with everybody. This is to be faithful in all God's house with good heart.

Like Moses who was faithful in all God's house

Moses was a prophet recognized by God to such an extent that God spoke to him face to face. Moses performed all his duties completely to accomplish the things God had commanded, not giving much thought to his own hardships. The people of Israel kept on complaining and disobeying when they faced a bit of difficulties even after having witnessed and experienced wonders and signs of God, but Moses continuously led them in faith and love. Even when God was angry with the people of Israel because of their sins, Moses did not turn away from them. He returned to the LORD, and said as the following:

> *Alas, this people has committed a great sin, and they have made a god of gold for themselves. But now, if You will, forgive their sin and if not, please blot me out from Your book which You have written! (Exodus 32:31-32)*

He fasted on behalf of the people, risking his own life, and was faithful more than God expected him to be. That is why God recognized and ensured Moses, saying, *"He is faithful in all My household"* (Numbers 12:7).

Furthermore, faithfulness that sardonyx symbolizes is to be faithful even to the point of death as written in Revelation 2:10. It is possible only when we love God first. It is giving all our time and money, and even life and doing more than what we are supposed to do with all our hearts and minds.

In old days, there were loyal retainers who assisted the king and were faithful to their nation, even to the point of sacrificing their own lives. If the king were a tyrant, truly loyal retainers would advise the king to follow the right way, even if this could easily have resulted in sacrificing their lives. They could have been exiled or put to death, but they were loyal because they loved the king and the nation even if that love were to claim their lives.

We must love God first to do more than what is asked of us, the way those loyal retainers gave up their lives for the nation, and the way Moses was faithful in all God's household to accomplish God's kingdom and righteousness. Thus, we are to sanctify ourselves quickly and be faithful in all the aspects of our lives so that we will have qualifications to enter New Jerusalem.

Sardius: Passionate Love

Sardius has a transparent, dark red color and symbolizes the blazing sun. It is the sixth foundation of the walls of New Jerusalem and spiritually symbolizes passion, enthusiasm, and passionate love in accomplishing God's kingdom and righteousness. It is the heart to faithfully execute given tasks and duties with all our strength.

Different levels of passionate love

There are many levels of love and generally, it can be divided into spiritual love and fleshly love. Spiritual love never changes because it is given from God, but fleshly love changes easily mainly because it is selfish.

No matter how true the love of worldly people may be, it can never be spiritual love, which is the love of the Lord that can only be acquired in the truth. We cannot have the spiritual love as soon as we accept the Lord and come to know the truth. We can obtain it only after we accomplish the heart of the Lord.

Do you have this spiritual love? You can examine yourself with the definition of spiritual love found in 1 Corinthians 13:4-7.

> *Love is patient, love is kind and is not jealous; love does not brag and is not arrogant, does not act unbecomingly; it does not seek its own, is not provoked, does not take into account a wrong suffered, does not rejoice in unrighteousness, but rejoices with the truth; bears all things, believes all things, hopes all things, endures all things.*

For example, if we are patient but selfish, or not easily angered but rude, we do not yet have the spiritual love of which Paul writes; we must not miss one single thing to have true spiritual love.

On the one hand, if you still have a sense of loneliness or void even though you think you have spiritual love, this is because you have wanted to receive something in return without realizing it. Your heart has not yet been filled with the truth of spiritual love completely.

On the other hand, if you are filled with spiritual love, you will never feel lonely or empty, but always be glad, happy, and thankful. Spiritual love rejoices in giving: the more you give, the more glad, grateful, and happy you will be.

Spiritual love rejoices in giving itself

Romans 5:8 tells us, *"But God demonstrates His own love toward us, in that while we were yet sinners, Christ died for us."*

God loves Jesus, His one and only Son, so much because Jesus is the truth itself that precisely resembles God Himself. Yet, He still gave His one and only Son as an atoning sacrifice. How great and precious God's love is!

God demonstrated His love for us by sacrificing His one and only Son. That is why it reads in 1 John 4:16, *"We have come to know and have believed the love which God has for us. God is love, and the one who abides in love abides in God, and God abides in him."*

In order to enter New Jerusalem, we must have God's love with which we can sacrifice ourselves, and which rejoices in giving so that we can produce the evidence that testifies to our life in God.

The apostle Paul's passionate love for souls

The very biblical figure that has this kind of passionate heart like sardius in devoting himself to the kingdom of God is the apostle Paul. From the time he met the Lord until the moment of his death his deeds of loving the Lord had never changed. As the apostle for the Gentiles, he saved many souls and established many churches through the three missionary trips. Until he was martyred in Rome, he constantly testified to Jesus Christ.

As the apostle of the Gentiles, Paul's way was very hard and perilous. He had many life-threatening situations and there were persecutions from the Jews continuously. He was beaten up and was jailed, and he was ship-wrecked three times. He went without sleep, he was often hungry and thirsty and he endured both cold and hot weather. During his missionary trips, there were always many situations that were difficult for a man to bear.

Nevertheless, Paul never regretted his choice. He never had any momentary thoughts like, 'It's difficult and I want to rest if only for a little while...' His heart was never swayed, and he never feared anything. Though he was going through so many troubles, his primary concern was only for the church and the believers.

It is just as he confessed in 2 Corinthians 11:28-29, *"Apart from such external things, there is the daily pressure on me of concern for all the churches. Who is weak without my being weak? Who is led into sin without my intense concern?"*

Until he finally gave up even his life, Paul showed passion and fervor as he endeavored for the salvation of souls. We can see how passionate his desire was for the salvation of souls in Romans 9:3, which reads, *"For I could wish that I myself were accursed, separated from Christ for the sake of my brethren, my kinsmen according to the flesh."*

Here, 'my brethren' is not just his blood relatives. It referred to all the Israelites, including the Jews who persecuted him. He said he could even choose to go to hell only if they could receive salvation. We can see how great his passionate love was for the souls and how great his fervor was for their salvation.

This passionate love for the Lord, the fervor and endeavor for salvation of other souls is represented by the red color of sardius.

Chrysolite: Mercy

Chrysolite, the seventh foundation of the walls of New Jerusalem, is a transparent or semi-transparent stone that gives out a yellow, green, blue, and pink color or seems at times completely transparent.

What does chrysolite symbolize spiritually? The spiritual meaning of mercy is to understand in truth somebody who cannot be understood at all and to forgive in truth a person who cannot be forgiven at all. To understand and forgive 'in truth' is to understand and forgive with love in goodness. The mercy, with which we can embrace others with love, is the mercy that is symbolized by chrysolite.

Those who have this mercy do not have any prejudice. They don't think, 'I don't like him because of this. I don't like her because of that.' They don't dislike or hate anybody. Of course, they don't have any enmity.

They just try to look at and think everything in a beautiful way. They just embrace everybody. So, even when they face a person who has committed a grave sin, they only show compassion. They hate the sin, but not the sinner. They rather understand him and embrace him. This is mercy.

The heart of mercy revealed through Jesus and Stephen

Jesus showed His mercy to Judas Iscariot who would sell Him out. Jesus knew from the beginning that Judas Iscariot would betray Him. Nevertheless, Jesus did not exclude him or keep His distance from him. He did not dislike or hate him in His heart either. Jesus loved him until the very end and He gave Judas chances to turn back. This heart is the merciful heart.

Even when Jesus was nailed on the cross, He did not complain against or hate anybody. He rather prayed in intercession for those who were inflicting pain and injury on Him, as recorded in Luke 23:34, which reads, *"Father, forgive them; for they do not know what they are doing."*

Stephen also had this kind of mercy. Though Stephen was not an apostle, he was full of grace and power. Evil people envied him and finally stoned him to death. But even while he was being stoned, he rather prayed for those who were killing him. It is recorded in Acts 7:60, *"Then falling on his knees, he cried out with a loud voice, 'Lord, do not hold this sin against them!' Having said this, he fell asleep."*

The fact that Stephen prayed for those who were killing him proves that he had already forgiven them. He didn't have any hatred against them. It shows us that he had the perfect fruit of mercy to have compassion on those people.

If there is anybody whom you hate or you don't like from among your family members or brothers in faith or colleagues at work, or there is anybody of whom you think, 'I don't like his attitude. He always opposes me, and I don't like him,' or if you just dislike and stay away from a person for various reasons, how far is it from 'mercy'?

We should not have anybody whom we dislike or hate. We should be able to understand, accept, and show goodness to everybody. God the Father shows us the beauty of mercy with the jewel, chrysolite.

A merciful heart that embraces everything

What, then, is the difference between love and mercy?

Spiritual love is sacrificing oneself without seeking his own interests or benefits, and not wanting anything in return, while mercy places more weight on forgiveness and tolerance. In other words, mercy is the heart that understands and does not hate even the ones who cannot be understood or loved. Mercy does not hate or scorn anybody but strengthens and comforts others. If you have this kind of warm heart, you will not point out others' faults and mistakes but instead embrace them so that you can have good relationships with them.

How, then, are we to act towards evil people? We must remember that we once were all evil, but came to God because somebody else had led us to the truth in love and forgiveness.

Also, when we come in contact with liars, we often forget that we, too, used to lie in pursuit of our own benefits before we believed in God. Instead of avoiding such people, we ought to show our mercy so that they may turn back from their wicked ways. Only when we understand and lead them with tolerance and love, can they realize the truth, and be changed and come into the truth. Likewise, mercy is treating everybody the same without any prejudice, not offending anyone, and trying to understand everything in a good way whether you like it or not.

Beryl: Patience

Beryl, the eighth foundation of the walls of New Jerusalem, has a blue or dark green color and reminds us of the blue sea. What does beryl spiritually symbolize? It symbolizes the patience in everything in accomplishing God's kingdom and His righteousness. Beryl stands for persevering in love, even the ones who persecute, curse, and hate you and not hating, quarreling, or fighting against them back.

James 5:10 urges us as follows: *"As an example, brethren, of suffering and patience, take the prophets who spoke in the name of the Lord."* We can change others when we are patient with them.

Patience as a fruit of the Holy Spirit and of spiritual love

We can read about patience as one of the nine fruits of the Holy Spirit in Galatians 5, and as a fruit of love in 1 Corinthians 13. Is there a difference between patience as a fruit of the Holy Spirit and patience as a fruit of love?

On the one hand, the patience in love refers to patience required in enduring any kind of personal strife, such as being patient with those who insult you or many kinds of hardships you encounter in life. On the other hand, patience as a fruit of the Holy Spirit refers to patience in truth and patience before God in *everything*.

Therefore, patience as a fruit of the Holy Spirit has a broader meaning, including patience about personal matters and matters relating to God's kingdom and His righteousness.

Different sorts of patience in truth

The patience to accomplish the kingdom and righteousness of God can be categorized into three kinds.

First, there is patience between God and us. We have to be patient until the promise of God is fulfilled. God the Father is faithful; once He has spoken something, He surely does it without reversing it. Thus, if we have received a promise from God, we have to be patient until it is fulfilled.

Also, if we have asked God something, we have to be patient until the answer comes. Some believers say as the following, "I pray all-night and even fast, and still there is no answer." This is just like a farmer who sows the seed and soon digs up the ground because there is no fruit immediately. If we have sown the seed, we have to be patient until it sprouts, grows up, blossoms with the flower and then bears the fruit.

A farmer pulls out the weeds and protects the crops from harmful insects. He does a lot of work with much sweat to gain good fruit. In the same way, to receive the answer to what we have prayed, we have things that have to be done. We have to fulfill the proper measure according to the measure of the seven Spirits—faith, joy, prayer, thanks, hard-working faithfulness, keeping the commandments, and love.

God answers us immediately only if we fulfill the required amounts according to measures for our faith. We have to understand that the time of patience with God is the time to receive a more perfect answer, and let us rejoice and give thanks even more.

Secondly, there is patience between men. The patience of spiritual love belongs to patience of this kind. To love any person in all kinds of human relationships, we need patience.

We need patience to believe in any kind of person, endure with him, and hope that he will prosper. Even if he does something that is opposite of what we have expected, we have to be patient in all things. We have to understand, be accepting, forgive, yield, and be patient.

Those who try to evangelize many people are likely to have some experiences of being cursed and persecuted. But if they patience in heart, they visit those souls again with smiles on their faces. With love to save those souls, they rejoice and give thanks, and never give up. When they show this kind of patience with goodness and love for a person who is being evangelized, the darkness goes away from him because of that light and the person can open his heart, accept it, and receive salvation.

Thirdly, there is patience to change the heart.

To change our heart is to pull out untruths and evil from our heart and to plant truth and goodness instead. To change our heart is similar to clearing a field. We have to remove the rocks and pull out the weeds. Sometimes, we have to plow the soil. Then, it can become a good field, and whatever we sow, it will grow and bear fruit.

It's the same with men's hearts. To the extent that we find evil in our heart and cast it off, we can have good fields of the heart. Then, when the Word of God is sown, it can sprout, grow well, and bear fruit. And just as we have to sweat and work hard to clear land, we have to do the same when we change our heart. We have to cry out earnestly in prayer with all our strength and with all our heart. Then we can receive the power of the Holy Spirit to plow the fleshly heart that is like barren land.

This process is not as easy as one might think. That is why some people may feel burdensome, get disheartened, or fall into despair. Therefore, we need patience. Even though it seems that we are changing very slowly, we should never be disappointed or give up.

We should remember the love of the Lord who died on the cross for us, receive new strength, and keep on cultivating the field of the heart. Also, we should look up to the love and blessings of God that He will give to us when we will have completely cultivated our heart. We should also keep on working with greater thanks.

If we had no evil in us, the term "patience" would not be

necessary. By the same token, if we only had love, forgiveness, and understanding, there would not be room for "patience." Thus, God wants us to have the kind of patience in which the word "patience" is not necessary. In fact, God, who Himself is goodness and love, does not need to be patient. Yet, He tells us He is "patient" with us to help us understand the concept of "patience." We are to realize that the more attributes we have to be patient with under certain circumstances, the more evil in God's sight we have in our own hearts.

If we have nothing to be patient with after accomplishing the perfect fruit of patience, we will always be happy, hear only the good tidings from here and there, and feel so light in our hearts as if we were walking on the clouds.

Topaz: Spiritual Goodness

Topaz, the ninth foundation of the walls of New Jerusalem, is a stone of a transparent, blend, and reddish orange color. The spiritual heart symbolized by topaz is spiritual goodness. Goodness is the quality of being kind, helpful, and honest. But spiritual meaning of goodness has deeper meaning.

There is goodness among the nine fruits of the Holy Spirit, too, and it has the same meaning with the goodness of topaz. The spiritual meaning of goodness is to seek goodness within the Holy Spirit.

Each person has a standard to judge between the right and the wrong or between good and evil. It is called "conscience." The concept of the conscience differs with diverse times, countries, and peoples.

The standard to measure the magnitude of spiritual goodness is only one: the Word of God, which is the truth. Therefore, to seek goodness from our perspective is not spiritual goodness. To seek the goodness in God's sight is spiritual goodness.

Matthew 12:35 says, *"The good man brings out of his good treasure what is good."* Likewise, those who have spiritual goodness in them will naturally bring out that goodness. Wherever they go and whomever they meet, good words and good deeds will come out from them.

Just as those who spray perfume will have a pleasant aroma, the aroma of goodness will come out from those who have goodness. Namely, they give out the aroma of the goodness of the Christ. Therefore, just by seeking goodness in heart cannot be called goodness. If we have the heart that seeks goodness, then we will naturally give out the aroma of the Christ with good words and deeds. This way, we should show moral virtue and love to people around us. This is goodness in true, spiritual sense.

The standard to measure spiritual goodness

God Himself is good, and goodness is found throughout the Bible, the Word of God. There are also verses in the Bible that specifically give out more of the colors of topaz, namely the colors of spiritual goodness.

First of all, it is found in Philippians 2:1-4, which reads, *"Therefore if there is any encouragement in Christ, if there is any consolation of love, if there is any fellowship of the Spirit, if any affection and compassion, make my joy complete by being of the same mind, maintaining the same love, united in spirit, intent on one purpose. Do nothing from selfishness or empty conceit, but with humility of mind regard one another as more important than yourselves; do not merely look out for your own personal interests, but also for the interests of others."*

Even though something is not right according to our thoughts and our characters, if we seek goodness in the Lord, we will bond with others and agree with their opinions. We will not quarrel in anything. We will not have any desire to flaunt ourselves or be lifted up by others. With only humble hearts, we will consider others better than us from the depths of our hearts. We will do our work faithfully and in a very responsible way. We will even be able to help others with their work.

We can easily see what kind of person has goodness in his heart from the parable of a good Samaritan found in Luke 10:25-37:

A man was going down from Jerusalem to Jericho, and fell among robbers, and they stripped him and beat him, and went away leaving him half dead. And by chance a priest was going down on that road, and when he saw him, he passed by on the other side. Likewise a Levite also, when he came to the place and saw him, passed by on the other side. But a Samaritan, who was on a journey, came upon him; and when he saw him, he felt compassion, and came to him and bandaged up his wounds, pouring oil and wine on them and he put him on his own beast, and brought him to an inn and took care of him. On the next day he took out two denarii and gave them to the innkeeper and said, "Take care of him; and whatever more you spend, when I return I will repay you." Which of these three do you think proved to be a neighbor to the man who fell into the robbers' hands? (Luke 10:30-36).

Among the priest, the Levite, and the Samaritan, who, then, is a true neighbor and a person of love? The Samaritan could be the true neighbor of the man who was robbed because he had goodness in his heart to choose the right way, even though he was considered as a Gentile.

This Samaritan might not have known the Word of God very well as knowledge. But we can see that he had the heart that followed goodness. It means he had the spiritual goodness following the goodness in God's sight. Even though we have to spend our own time and money, we have to choose the goodness in God's sight. This is spiritual goodness.

Jesus' goodness

Another Bible verse that gives out the light of goodness more brightly is Matthew 12:19-20. It is concerned with the goodness of Jesus. It reads:

> *He will not quarrel, nor cry out; nor will anyone hear His voice in the streets. A battered reed He will not break off, and a smoldering wick He will not put out, until He leads justice to victory.*

The phrase "until He leads justice to victory" emphasizes that Jesus acted only with a good heart in the entire process of crucifixion and resurrection, giving us victory with His grace of salvation.

Since Jesus had spiritual goodness, He never offended or quarreled with anybody. He accepted everything with the wisdom of spiritual goodness and words of truth even when He encountered harsh and seemingly unacceptable situations.

Moreover, Jesus neither confronted the ones who tried to kill Him nor attempted to explain and prove His innocence. He left everything to God and accomplished everything with His wisdom and truth in spiritual goodness.

Spiritual goodness is the heart that "should not break off a bruised reed or put out a smoldering wick." This definition holds the representative reference points of goodness.

Those who have goodness do not cry out or quarrel with anybody. Also, they will show their goodness in their appearances as well. As recorded, "Nor will anyone hear His voice in the streets," those who have goodness will give out goodness and humbleness on the outside. How blameless and perfect must Jesus' habits have been in His manner of walking, gestures, and language! Proverbs 22:11 says, *"He who loves purity of heart and whose speech is gracious, the king is his friend."*

First, a 'bruised reed' represents those who suffered many things of this world and are hurt in their heart. Even when they seek God with a poor heart, God will not forsake them, but accept them. This heart of God and this heart of Jesus is the very height of goodness.

Next, it's the same with the heart that does not snuff out a smoldering wick. If the wick is smoldering, it means the fire is dying, but there still is the kindling that remains. In this sense, 'a smoldering wick' is a person who is so stained with evil that the light of his spirit is 'smoldering.' Even this kind of person, if he has the slightest possibility of receiving salvation, we should not give up on him. This is goodness.

Our Lord does not give up on even those people who live in sins and stand against God. He still knocks on the door of their heart to allow for them to reach salvation. This heart of our Lord is goodness.

There are people who are like bruised reeds and smoldering wicks in faith. When they fall to temptations because of weak faith, some people don't have the strength to come back to church again by themselves. Maybe because of some fleshly things that they have not cast off yet, they might have caused damage to other church members. Because they are so sorry and embarrassed about it, they don't feel they can return to the church.

So we have to first go to them. We have to extend our hands to them and hold their hands. This is goodness. Also, there are people who were first in faith, but later are behind in spirit. Some of them also become like the 'smoldering wick'.

Some of them want to be loved and recognized by others, but it doesn't happen. So they are heartbroken and the evil in them comes out. They may be jealous of others who are going ahead in spirit, and they may even slander them. This is like the smoldering wick that is giving out smoke and fumes.

If we have true goodness, we will also be able to understand these people and accept them. If we try to discuss what is right and wrong and make the other people submit, it is not goodness. We have to treat them well with truthfulness and love, even those who show evil. We have to melt and move their hearts. When we do this it is acting in goodness.

Chrysoprase: Self-control

Chrysoprase, the tenth foundation of the walls of the New Jerusalem, is the most expensive among chalcedonies. It is of a semi-transparent dark green color, and one of the precious stones

Korean women used to consider very valuable in old days. To them it symbolized chastity and purity of women.

What does chrysoprase symbolize spiritually? It stands for self-control. It is good to have abundance in everything in God, but there must be self-control to make everything beautiful. Self-control is also one of the nine fruits of the Holy Spirit.

Self-control to accomplish perfection

Titus 1:7-9 tells us about the conditions of an overseer of a church, and one of the conditions is self-control. If a person who lacks self-control becomes an overseer, what would he be able to accomplish in his uncontrolled life?

In whatever we do for and in the Lord, we should tell apart the truth from untruth, and follow the will of the Holy Spirit with self-control. If we are able to hear the voice of the Holy Spirit, we will be prosperous in all things since we have self-control. If we do not have self-control, however, things may go wrong and we might even encounter accidents, both natural and man-made disasters, diseases, and the like.

Likewise, the fruit of self-control is so important, and it is a must in accomplishing the perfection. As much as we bear the fruit of love, we can bear the fruit of joy, peace, patience, kindness, goodness, faithfulness, and gentleness, and these fruit will be complete with self-control.

Self-control can be compared to the anus in our body. Though it is small, it plays a very important role in the body. What if it loses the strength to contract? Excrements will not be controlled, and we will be all but dirty and indecent.

In the same way, if we lose our self-control, everything may turn out to be messy. People live in untruth because they cannot control themselves spiritually. Because of that, they face trials and cannot be loved by God. If we cannot control ourselves physically, we will be doing unrighteous and unlawful things because we will eat and get drunk as much as we want, making our lives disorderly.

John the Baptist

A good example of self control among the biblical figures is John the Baptist.

John the Baptist clearly knew why he came to this earth. He knew that he had to prepare the way for Jesus, who is the true Light. So, until he fulfilled this duty, he lived a completely secluded life from this world. He armed himself with prayer and the Word alone while in the wilderness. He ate only locusts and wild honey. It was a very secluded and strictly controlled life. Through this kind of life, he was ready to prepare the way of the Lord, and fulfilled it completely.

In Matthew 11:11, Jesus said this about him, *"Truly I say to you, among those born of women there has not arisen anyone greater than John the Baptist!"*

If somebody thinks, 'Oh, so now I will go to deep into the mountains or some secluded place and live a life with self-control!' this proves that he doesn't have self-control and interprets God's Word in his own way and thinks too much.

It is important to control your heart in the Holy Spirit. If you have not yet reached the level of spirit, you have to control your fleshly desires and follow only the desires of the Holy Spirit. Also, even after you accomplish spirit, you have to control the strength or magnitude of each of the spiritual hearts to have perfect harmony as a whole. This self-control is shown with the light of chrysoprase.

Jacinth: Purity and Holiness

Jacinth, the eleventh foundation of the walls of New Jerusalem, is a precious stone of a transparent, bluish color and spiritually symbolizes purity and holiness.

"Purity" here refers to a state of having no sin and being clean without any spot and blemish. If a person takes a shower or bath a couple of times a day, combs his hair and dresses neatly, people will say he is clean and neat. Then, would God say he is clean, too? Who, then, is a man with a pure heart and how can we accomplish the pure heart?

A pure heart in the sight of God

The Pharisees and the scribes washed their hands before they ate, following the traditions of the elders. And when the disciples of Jesus didn't do so, they asked Jesus a question to accuse Him. Matthew 15:2 says, *"Why do Your disciples break the tradition of the elders? For they do not wash their hands when they eat bread."*

Jesus taught them what purity really is. In Matthew 15:19-20 He said, *"For out of the heart come evil thoughts, murders, adulteries, fornications, thefts, false witness, slanders. These are the things which defile the man; but to eat with unwashed hands does not defile the man."*

The purity in the sight of God is to have no sin in the heart. Purity is when we have a heart that is clean having no blame, spot, or blemish. We can wash our hands and body with water, but how can we purify our heart?

We can also wash it with water. We can purify it by washing it with the spiritual water that is the Word of God. Hebrews 10:22 says, *"let us draw near with a sincere heart in full assurance of faith, having our hearts sprinkled clean from an evil conscience and our bodies washed with pure water."* We can have clean and true hearts to the extent that we act according to the Word of God.

When we obey whatever the Bible tells us to cast away and not to do, the untruth and evil will be washed from our heart. And when we obey whatever the Bible commands us to do and keep, we can avoid being stained by the sins and evil of the world again by constantly being supplied with the clean water. This way we can keep our heart clean.

Matthew 5:8 says, *"Blessed are the pure in heart, for they shall see God."* God has told us about the blessing the pure in heart will receive. It is that they will see God. Those who are pure in heart will see God face to face in the kingdom of heaven. They can go into at least the Third Kingdom of heaven or even enter into New Jerusalem.

But the real meaning of 'seeing God' is not just seeing God. It means that we always meet with God and receive help from Him. It means we are living a life in which we walk with God, even on this earth.

Enoch who accomplished pure heart

The fifth chapter of Genesis depicts Enoch who cultivated pure heart and walked with God on earth. In Genesis 5:21-24, we can read that Enoch walked with God three hundred years from the time when he became the father of Methuselah at 65. Then, as recorded in verse 4, *"Enoch walked with God; and he was not, for God took him,"* he was taken up to heaven alive.

Hebrews 11:5 tells us the reason why he could be caught up to Heaven without seeing death, which says, *"By faith Enoch was taken up so that he would not see death; and he was not found because God took him up; for he obtained the witness that before his being taken up he was pleasing to God."*

Enoch pleased God by cultivating such a pure heart without having any sin, even to the extent that he didn't have to see death. And finally he was taken up to heaven alive. He was 365 at that time, but in those days people used to live for more than 900 years. In today's sense, God took Enoch when he was at the most vigorous time of youth.

It was because Enoch was so lovely in God's eyes. Rather than to keep him on the earth, God wanted to set Enoch close to His side in the heavenly kingdom. We can clearly see how much God loves and rejoices over those who have pure hearts.

But even Enoch did not just become sanctified overnight. He also went through various kinds of trials until he was 65. In Genesis 5:19, we can see that Jared, the father of Enoch, gave birth to children for 800 years following Enoch's birth, so we can understand that Enoch had many brothers and sisters.

God has let me know in deep prayers that Enoch had no trouble whatsoever with any of his brothers and sisters. He never wanted to have more than his brothers; he always made concessions to them. He never wanted to be recognized more than his brothers and sisters, and he only did his best. Even when some other brothers were loved more than he, Enoch didn't have any discomfort, which means he didn't have any jealousy.

Also, Enoch was always an obedient person. He listened to not only to the Word of God, but also to the word of his parents. He never insisted on his own opinion. He didn't have any self-centered desires, and didn't take anything personally. He lived at peace with everybody.

Enoch cultivated a pure heart in him with which he could see God. When Enoch became 65, he reached the level to please God, and he could now walk with God.

But there is a more important reason why he could walk with God. That is because he loved God and enjoyed communicating with God very much. Of course he did not set his eyes upon the things of this world and he loved God more than anything of this world.

Enoch loved his parents and obeyed them, and there was peace and love between him and all his siblings, yet it was God he loved the most. He enjoyed being alone and praising God more than remaining with his family members. He missed God as he watched the sky and the nature, and enjoyed the communion he had with God.

It was so even before God began to walk with him, and from the time God began to walk with him, it was even more so. As recorded in Proverbs 8:17 that says, *"I love those who love me; and those who diligently seek me will find me,"* Enoch loved God and missed Him so much, and God also walked with him.

The more we love God, the purer the heart will become, and the purer the heart we have, the more we will love God and seek Him. It is comfortable to talk and interact with those who are pure in heart. They just accept everything purely and believe others.

Who would feel bad and frown seeing the bright smiles of little babies? Most people would feel good and also smile when they see babies. It's because the purity of the babies is passed on to the people, refreshing their hearts, too.

God the Father feels in the same way when He sees a person with a pure heart. So, He wants to see this kind of person more and He would want to stay with him.

Amethyst: Beauty and Gentleness

The twelfth and last foundation of the walls of New Jerusalem is amethyst. Amethyst has light violet color and is transparent. Amethyst has such an elegant and beautiful color that it has been loved by the nobles since ancient times.

God also deems the spiritual heart symbolized by amethyst as beautiful. The spiritual heart amethyst symbolizes is gentleness. This gentleness is found in the Chapter on Love, in the Beatitudes, and even in the nine fruits of the Holy Spirit. It is a fruit that is surely borne in a person who gives birth to spirit through the Holy Spirit and lives by the Word of God.

The heart of gentleness deemed beautiful by God

A dictionary defines gentleness as the characters of kindness, mildness, and meekness; [and] being able to impart calmness. But the gentleness God deems beautiful is not just those characters.

Those who have gentle characters in flesh feel somewhat uncomfortable about people who are not gentle. When they see somebody who is very outgoing or strong in character, they become somewhat cautious, and they even feel it difficult to interact with that kind of person. But a person who is spiritually gentle can accept any kind of person of any kind of character. This is one of the differences between fleshly gentleness and spiritual gentleness.

Then, what is the spiritual gentleness, and why does God consider it beautiful?

To be spiritually gentle is to have a mild and warm character along with a broad heart to accept everybody. It is somebody who possesses the heart that is soft and cozy as cotton so that many people can find rest in him. Also, it's somebody who can understand everything in goodness and embrace and accept everything in love.

And there is one thing that cannot be missing in spiritual gentleness. It is the virtuous character in relation with having a broad heart. If we have very warm and soft heart only within ourselves, it doesn't really mean anything. From time to time, when it's necessary, we should be able to encourage and give advice to others, showing deeds of goodness and love. To show virtuous character is to strengthen others, let them feel the warmth, and let them find rest in our heart.

A spiritually gentle person

Those who have true spiritual gentleness do not have any prejudice about any person. So, they don't have any trouble and they are not on bad terms with anybody. The other person also feels this warm heart, so he can take rest and find peace of mind feeling he is embraced very warmly. This spiritual gentleness is like a big tree that provides a big, cool shadow on a hot summer day.

If the husband accepts and embraces all his family members with a broad heart, the wife will respect and love him. If the wife also has a heart that is soft like cotton, she can provide comfort and peace to her husband, so they can be a very happy couple. Also, those children who are raised in such a family will not go astray even when they are faced with difficulties. Because they can be strengthened in the peacefulness of the family, they can overcome difficulties and grow up with uprightness and in good health.

Likewise, through those who have cultivated spiritual gentleness, people around them can also find rest and feel happy. Then, God the Father will also say those who are spiritually gentle are really beautiful.

In this world people implement various ways to gain the heart of others. They may supply others with material things or use their social fame or authority. But with those fleshly ways, we cannot truly gain the hearts of others. They may help us for the moment because of their needs, but because they don't really submit from the heart, they will change their mind when the situations change.

But people will naturally gather around a person who has spiritual gentleness. They submit from their heart and desire to remain with him. It's because, through a person who has spiritual gentleness, they can be strengthened and feel the comfort that they couldn't feel in the world. So, many people will stay with a person with spiritual gentleness, and this becomes the spiritual authority.

Matthew 5:5 speaks about this blessing of gaining many souls saying that they will inherit the earth. It means they will gain the heart of men who are made from earth. As a result, they will also receive a large area of land in the eternal heavenly kingdom. Because they have embraced and guided many souls to the truth, they will receive much reward.

That's why God said this about Moses in Numbers 12:3, *"Now the man Moses was very humble, more than any man who was on the face of the earth."* Moses led the Exodus. He led more than 2 million people, and guided them for 40 years in the wilderness. Just as parents raise their children, he embraced them in his heart and guided them according to the will of God.

Even when their children commit grave sins, the parents will not just desert them. In the same way, Moses harbored even those people who could not help but be forsaken according to the Law, and he guided them until the end asking God to forgive them.

When you have even just a minor duty in the church, you will understand how good this gentleness is. Not only in duties of taking care of the souls, but in any kind of duty, if you do it with gentleness, you will have no problem. There are no two people who have the same heart and same thoughts. Everybody has been raised in different circumstances and has different characters. Their thoughts and opinions may not agree.

But he who is gentle can accept others with a broad heart. The gentleness to empty oneself and accept others stands out beautifully in a situation where everyone insists that he is right.

We have learned about all the spiritual hearts symbolized by each of the twelve foundation stones of the city wall of New Jerusalem. They are the hearts of faith, uprightness, sacrifice, righteousness, faithfulness, passion, mercy, patience, goodness, self-control, purity, and gentleness. When we consolidate all these characters, it becomes the heart of Jesus Christ and God the Father. In one phrase, it is 'perfect love'.

Those who have cultivated this perfect love with a good and balanced combination of each character of the twelve jewels can boldly enter into the City of New Jerusalem. Also, their houses in New Jerusalem will be adorned with the twelve different jewels.

Therefore, the inside of the City of New Jerusalem is so beautiful and enrapturing beyond expression. The houses, buildings, and all facilities like parks are decorated in the most beautiful way possible.

But what God deems the most beautiful is the people who come into the City. They will give out more brilliant lights than the lights coming out from all twelve jewels. They will also give out thick aroma of love toward the Father from the depth of their hearts. Through this, God the Father will be comforted for all the things He will have done by then.

Chapter 6

The Twelve Pearl Gates
and the Golden Road

"And the twelve gates were twelve pearls;
each one of the gates was a single pearl.
the street of the city was pure gold,
like transparent glass."

- Revelation 21:21

The City of New Jerusalem has twelve gates, three each on north, south, east and west side of its walls. An enormous angel guards each gate, and the sight displays the magnificence and the authority of the City of New Jerusalem at a glance. Each gate is arch-shaped, and it is so enormous that we have to look far up. Each gate is made of one gigantic pearl. It slides open to either side and has a handle made of gold and other precious stones. The gate opens automatically without someone having to open it by hands.

God has made twelve gates with beautiful pearls and the streets with pure gold for His beloved children. How much more beautiful and gorgeous would the structures in the City be?

Before we delve into the buildings and sites in the City of New Jerusalem, let us first consider the reasons God has made the gates of New Jerusalem with pearls, and what kind of streets there are other than the golden streets.

The Twelve Gates Made of Pearl

Revelation 21:21 reads, *"And the twelve gates were twelve pearls; each one of the gates was a single pearl. And the street of the city was pure gold, like transparent glass."* Why, then, are the twelve gates made of pearls while there are many other precious stones in New Jerusalem? Some may say it would be better to decorate each gate with different jewels since there are twelve gates, but God has adorned all twelve gates only with pearl.

This is because there are God's providence and spiritual significance contained in this design. Unlike other jewels, pearls hold a somewhat different value and are thus deemed more precious because they are produced after a painful process.

Why are the twelve gates made with pearls?

How is a pearl produced? Pearl is one of the two organic jewels from the sea, the other being coral. It has been widely adored by countless people since it gives out a beautiful gloss without having to be polished.

Pearl is formed on the inner skin of the shell of an oyster. It is a lump of abnormal glossy discharge consisting mainly of calcium carbonate, in a semi-sphere or sphere shape. When foreign substance gets into the soft flesh of the shell, the shell suffers from a great pain, as if a needle were pricking it. Then, the shell fights the foreign substance bearing a tremendous amount of pain. A pearl is produced when the discharge of the shell covers the foreign substance over and over again.

There are two kinds of pearl: natural pearls and cultivated pearls. People have figured out the principle in producing pearls. They raise many shells and insert artificial substances into the shells so that they will produce pearls. These pearls seemingly look natural but they are relatively cheaper because they have thinner pearl layers.

Just as a shell makes a beautiful pearl bearing great pain against foreign substances, there is a process of endurance for God's children striving to recover the lost image of God. They can come forth with faith like pure gold with which they can enter New Jerusalem only after they have endured hardships and sorrow while living on this earth.

If we want to win the victory in the fight of faith and pass through the gates of the City of New Jerusalem, we all have to make a pearl in our heart. Just as the pearl oyster endures with pain and secrets the nacre to make a pearl, God's children also have to endure with pain until they recover the image of God fully.

As sin came into the world and people became stained with sins more and more, they lost the image of God. In the heart of men were planted evil and untruth, and their hearts became unclean, giving out foul stench. God the Father showed His great love even to these people who were living with sinful hearts in sinful world.

Anybody who believes in Jesus Christ will be cleansed of his sin through His blood. But the kind of true children that God the Father wants is those children who are fully grown and matured. He wants those who will not get themselves dirty again after they are washed. Spiritually, it means they do not commit sins any more, but please the Father God with perfect faith.

And to have this kind of perfect faith, we first have to have true hearts. We can have a true heart when we remove all sins and evil from our heart and fill it with goodness and love instead. The more goodness and love we have, the more we have recovered the image of God.

God the Father allows refining trials to His children so that they can cultivate goodness and love. He lets them find out sins and evil in their hearts in various kinds of situations. When we find our sins and evil, we will feel the pain in our heart. It's like when a sharp intruder gets into an oyster and pierces into the soft flesh. But we have to acknowledge the fact that we have pain when we go through trials because of sins and evil in our heart.

If we really acknowledge this fact, we can now make a spiritual pearl in our heart. We will pray fervently to cast off the sins and evil we have discovered. Then, the grace and strength of God will come upon us. Also, the Holy Spirit will help us. As a result, the sins and evil we have found out will be removed, and instead, we will have spiritual heart.

Pearls are extremely precious when the process of producing them is considered. Just as shells have to suffer the pain and endure to produce pearls, we have to overcome and endure great pain to enter New Jerusalem. We can enter through these gates only when we gain the victory in the battle of faith. These gates are made to symbolize this fact.

Hebrews 12:4 tells us, *"You have not yet resisted to the point of shedding blood in your striving against sin."* And the second half of Revelation 2:10 also urges us to *"Be faithful until death, and I will give you the crown of life."*

As the Bible tells us, we can enter New Jerusalem, the most beautiful place in heaven, only when we resist sin, throw away all kinds of evil, are faithful even to the point of death, and fulfill our duties.

Overcoming trials of faith

We must have faith like pure gold to pass the twelve gates of New Jerusalem. This kind of faith is not just given; only when we pass and overcome the trials of faith are we rewarded such faith just as a shell bears great pain until it makes a pearl. Yet, it is not so easy to prevail with faith because there are the enemy devil and Satan who try to prevent us from having faith at all costs. Moreover, until we stand on the rock of faith, we might feel that the way to heaven is hard and painful because we have to face intense battles against the enemy devil as much as we have untruth in our hearts.

However, we can overcome because God gives us His grace and strength, and the Holy Spirit helps and guides us. If we stand on the rock of faith after following these steps, we will be able to overcome all kinds of hardships and rejoice instead of suffering.

Buddhist monks beat their bodies and "enslave" them through meditations to do away with all the worldly matters. Some of them practice asceticism for decades, and when they die, a pearl-like object from their remains is retrieved. This is formed after many years of endurance and self-control, the way pearls are made by oyster shells.

How much would we have to endure and control ourselves from pain if we tried to do away with worldly pleasures and control the lust of the body with our strength alone? Yet, God's children can do away with worldly pleasures quickly with the grace and strength of God in the midst of the works of the Holy Spirit. Also, we can overcome any kind of hardship with the help of God, and we can run the spiritual race because heaven is prepared for us.

Therefore, God's children who have faith do not have to endure their trials in pain, but overcome with joy and thanksgiving, anticipating the blessings that they are to receive soon enough.

Twelve pearl gates are for the victors in faith

The twelve pearl gates serve as triumphal arches for victors in faith, the way victorious commanders returning home after successful battles march through a monument honoring their feat.

In old days, to welcome and honor soldiers and their commanders returning home in triumph, people built various monuments and structures and named each site after heroic men. The triumphant general would be honored and go through a triumphal arch or gate, welcomed by a large crowd, riding on the wagon sent for by the king.

When they reach the banquet hall in the midst of triumphal singing, ministers who were sitting with the king and the queen welcome them. The commander then gets down from the wagon and bows down to his king, and the king would raise him up and praise his distinguished service. They then eat, drink, and share the joy of the victory. The commander might be rewarded authority, riches, and honors comparable to those of the king.

If the authority of a commander and the army is this great, how much greater would the authority of those who pass through the twelve gates of New Jerusalem be? They will be loved and comforted by the Father God and dwell there forever in the glory that cannot be compared to that of a commander or soldiers who go through any triumphal arch. When they pass through the twelve gates made wholly of pearl, they are reminded of their journey of faith during which they struggled and attempted their best, and shed tears surging from the depths of their hearts in gratitude.

Grandeur of the twelve pearl gates

In heaven, people never forget anything even after a long time because heaven is a part of the spiritual world. Instead, they sometimes cherish the time reminiscing the past.

That is why those who enter New Jerusalem are overwhelmed whenever they look at the twelve gates of pearl, thinking, 'I have overcome many trials and finally arrived at New Jerusalem!' They rejoice in remembering the fact that they struggled and finally won against the enemy devil and the world, and cast off any and all untruth in them. They give thanks to God the Father once again, remembering His love that led them to overcome the world. They also give thanks to the ones who helped them until they reached that place.

In this world, the degree of gratitude sometimes fades completely or diminishes as time goes by, but since there is no insincerity in heaven, people's gratitude, joy, and love grow more and more with the passing of time. Thus, whenever New Jerusalem residents look at the pearl gates, they are thankful for God's love and to the ones who had helped them get there.

Streets Made of Pure Gold

As people reminisce their lives on the earth and pass the majestic arch-shaped pearl gates, they finally enter New Jerusalem. The City is full of the light of God's glory, the distant, peaceful sound of angel's praise, and mild scents of the flowers. As they take each step into the City, they feel inexpressible happiness and rapture.

The walls adorned with twelve jewels and the beautiful pearl gates have already been discussed. Of what, then, are the streets in New Jerusalem made? As Revelation 21:21 tells us, *"And the street of the city was pure gold, like transparent glass,"* God made the streets of New Jerusalem with pure gold for His children who enter the City.

Jesus Christ: The Way

In this world, there are many kinds of roads, ranging from a hushed trail to railroads, from narrow streets to highways. Depending on the destination and the need, people take different paths. In order to go to heaven, however, there is only one way: Jesus Christ.

I am the way, and the truth, and the life; no one comes to the Father but through Me (John 14:6).

Jesus, the one and only Son of God, opened the way of salvation by being crucified on behalf of all men, who were to die forever because of their sins, and resurrecting on the third day. When we believe in Jesus Christ, we are qualified to receive eternal life. Therefore, Jesus Christ is the only way to heaven, salvation, and eternal life. Moreover, it is the way to eternal life to accept Jesus Christ and to resemble His nature.

Golden streets

On each side of the River of the Water of Life are streets that allow everyone to easily find the throne of God in the boundless heaven. The River of the Water of Life originates from the throne of God and the Lamb, flows through the City of New Jerusalem and all the dwelling places in heaven, and returns to the throne of God.

> *Then he showed me a river of the water of life, clear as crystal, coming from the throne of God and of the Lamb, in the middle of its street. On either side of the river was the tree of life, bearing twelve kinds of fruit, yielding its fruit every month; and the leaves of the tree were for the healing of the nations (Revelation 22:1-2).*

Spiritually, "water" symbolizes the Word of God, and because we gain life through His Word and go the way of eternal life through Jesus Christ, the Water of Life flows from the throne of God and of the Lamb.

Moreover, since the River of the Water of Life encircles heaven, we can reach New Jerusalem easily just by following the golden streets on each side of the River.

The significance of golden streets

Golden streets are laid not only in New Jerusalem, but also throughout all places in heaven. However, just as the brightness, materials, and beauty differ from each dwelling place to another, the brightness of the golden streets also differs in each dwelling place.

Pure gold in heaven, unlike gold found in this world, is not soft but firm. Yet, when we walk on these golden streets, it feels very soft. Moreover, in heaven there is no dust or anything dirty, and since nothing ever gets worn out, the golden streets never get damaged. On each side of the streets bloom beautiful flowers and they greet God's children walking on the streets.

What, then, is the significance and reason for making the

streets with pure gold? It is to remind us that the cleaner their hearts are, the better place within heaven they can reside. Furthermore, since we can enter New Jerusalem only when we advance towards the City with faith and hope, God has made the streets with pure gold, which stands for spiritual faith and the fervent hope born from this faith.

Flower roads

Just as there are differences in walking on the freshly mowed lawn, rocks, paved roads, and so forth, there is a difference between walking on the golden streets and flower roads. There are also other roads made of jewels, and there is a distinction in happiness felt when walking on them. We also notice the difference in comfort among various means of transportation such as airplane, train, or bus, and it is the same in heaven. Walking on the roads ourselves is wholly different from being transported automatically by God's power.

The flower roads in heaven do not have the flowers on each side of the roads because the roads themselves are made of flowers so that people can walk on the flowers. It feels soft and fluffy like walking on a soft rug in bare feet. The flowers do not get damaged or withered because our bodies are spiritual bodies that are very light, and the flowers are not trampled on.

Moreover, heavenly flowers rejoice and give out their scents when children of God walk on them. So when they walk on the flower roads, the scents are absorbed into their bodies so that their hearts will be blissful, refreshed, and happy.

Jewel roads

The roads are made of jewels with many kinds of brilliant colors and full of beautiful lights, and, what is more interesting, they shine more beautiful lights when spiritual bodies walk on them. Even the jewels give out scents, and the happiness and the joy felt are beyond comprehension. Also, we can feel a bit of thrill when walking on jewel roads because it feels like walking on water. Yet, this does not mean we would feel as if we were sinking into water or drowning, but instead feel ecstasy in each step with a bit of strain.

However, we can find roads of jewel only in certain places in heaven. In other words, they are rewarded in and around the house of those who resemble the heart of the Lord and had contributed a great deal in accomplishing God's providence of the human cultivation. It is like the way even a small passage is adorned with elegant decorations made of highest-quality materials in a king's castle or palace.

People do not grow tired of or fed up with anything in heaven but love everything forever because it is the spiritual world. Also, they feel more joy and happiness because even such a little object is embedded with spiritual significance, and people's love and admiration accordingly increase.

How beautiful and wonderful New Jerusalem is! It is prepared by God for his beloved children. Even the people in Paradise and the First, Second, and Third Kingdoms of Heaven greatly rejoice and become grateful when they pass through the pearl gates with invitation to New Jerusalem.

Can you imagine how much more the children of God would be grateful and joyful about the fact that they arrived at New

Jerusalem as a result of having faithfully followed the Lord, the true way?

Three keys to enter the City of New Jerusalem

New Jerusalem is a cubic-shaped city with its width, length, and height all 2,400 km. The city wall has a total of twelve gates and twelve foundation stones. The city wall, the twelve gates, and the twelve foundation stones have spiritual meanings. If we understand those meanings and accomplish them in our hearts, we can have the spiritual qualifications to enter into New Jerusalem. In this sense, those spiritual meanings are the keys to enter the City of New Jerusalem.

The first key to enter into New Jerusalem is hidden in the city wall. As recorded in Revelation 21:18, *"The material of the wall was jasper; and the city was pure gold, like clear glass,"* the city wall is made of jasper, which spiritually symbolizes the faith to please God.

Faith is the most basic and essential thing in Christian life. Without faith we cannot be saved and we cannot please God. To enter into the City of New Jerusalem, we have to have the faith to please God—the fifth level of faith, which is the highest level of faith. Therefore, the first key is the fifth level of faith—the faith to please God.

The second key is found in the twelve foundation stones. The consolidation of the spiritual hearts represented by the twelve foundation stones is the perfect love, and this perfect love is the second key to New Jerusalem.

The twelve foundations are made of twelve different jewels.

Each jewel on the twelve foundations symbolizes a specific kind of spiritual heart. They are the hearts of faith, uprightness, sacrifice, righteousness, faithfulness, passion, mercy, patience, goodness, self-control, purity, and gentleness. When we consolidate all these characters, it becomes the heart of Jesus Christ and God the Father who is love itself. In summation, the second key to go into New Jerusalem is perfect love.

The third key hidden in the City of New Jerusalem is twelve pearl gates. Through the pearl, God wants us to realize how we can go into New Jerusalem. Pearl is made very differently from other jewels. All of the gold, silver, and the precious gemstones that make up the 12 foundation stones, they all come from the earth. But pearl is uniquely made from a living thing.

Most pearls are made by pearl oysters. The pearl oyster endures with pain and secrets the nacre to make a pearl. In the same way, God's children also have to endure with pain until they recover the image of God fully.

God the Father wants to gain those children who do not get themselves dirty again after they are washed by the blood of Jesus Christ, but please the Father God with perfect faith. Possessing this perfect faith requires for us to have true heart. We can have a true heart when we remove all sins and evil from our heart and fill it with goodness and love instead.

That is why God allows us trials of faith until we have true heart and perfect faith. He lets us find out sins and evil in our hearts in various kinds of situations. When we find our sins and evil, we will feel the pain in our heart. It's like when a sharp intruder gets into an oyster and pierces into the soft flesh. Just in the same way that the pearl oyster covers the unwelcome intruder layer by layer with nacre adding thickness layer by layer, when we go through trials with faith, the nacre of our heart will become thicker. As a pearl oyster makes a pearl, we believers also have to make spiritual pearl to go into New Jerusalem. This is the third key to enter New Jerusalem.

I wish for you to understand the spiritual meanings embedded in the city wall of New Jerusalem, the twelve gates of the wall, and the twelve foundation stones, and to have the three keys to enter New Jerusalem by having spiritual qualifications.

 Chapter 7

The Charming Spectacle

"I saw no temple in it, for the Lord God the Almighty
and the Lamb are its temple.
And the city has no need of the sun
or of the moon to shine on it,
for the glory of God has illumined it,
and its lamp is the Lamb.
The nations will walk by its light,
and the kings of the earth will bring their glory into it.
In the daytime (for there will be no night there)
its gates will never be closed;
and they will bring the glory
and the honor of the nations into it;
and nothing unclean, and no one
who practices abomination and lying,
shall ever come into it,
but only those whose names are written
in the Lamb's book of life."

- Revelation 21:22-27

The apostle John, to whom the Holy Spirit showed New Jerusalem, recorded the sight of the City in detail while looking down at it from a higher place. John had long yearned to see the inside of New Jerusalem, and when he finally saw the interior of the City whose sight was so beautiful, it put him in an ecstatic state.

If we have the qualifications to enter New Jerusalem and stand before the gate, we will be able to see the arch-shaped pearl gate open, which itself is too large for us to see the ends of it.

At that moment, the inexpressibly beautiful lights from the City of New Jerusalem come forth and surround our bodies. We feel the great love of God in an instant and cannot control tears streaming down.

Feeling the overflowing love of God the Father who has protected us with His blazing eyes, the grace of the Lord who has forgiven us with His blood on the cross, and the love of the Holy Spirit dwelling in our hearts, who has led us to live in the truth, we give infinite glory and honor.

Let us now examine details of the City of New Jerusalem based on the account of the apostle John.

No Need for the Sunshine or the Moonlight

The apostle John, looking at the scenery of the inside of New Jerusalem that was filled with God's glory, confessed as follows:

And the city has no need of the sun or of the moon to shine on it, for the glory of God has illumined it, and its lamp is the Lamb (Revelation 21:23).

New Jerusalem is filled with God's glory since God Himself stays and rules over the City, and in it is the summit of the spiritual realm at which God formed Himself into the Trinity for the human cultivation.

God's glory shines on New Jerusalem

The reason that God has put the sun and the moon for this earth is for us to recognize good and evil, and distinguish spirit from flesh through the light and darkness so that we could live as true children of God. He knows everything about spirit and flesh, and good and evil, but human beings cannot realize these things without the human cultivation because they are mere creatures.

When the first man Adam was in the Garden of Eden before the beginning of the human cultivation, he could never come to know about evil, death, darkness, poverty, or disease. That is why he could not grasp true meaning and happiness of life or be thankful to God who had given him everything, even though his life was so abundant.

For this Adam to know true happiness, he needed to shed tears, mourn, suffer from pain and disease, and experience death, and this is the process of human cultivation. Please refer to *The Message of the Cross* for more detail.

Eventually, Adam committed the sin of disobedience by eating from the tree of the knowledge of good and evil, was driven out to this earth, and came to experience the relativity. Only after that could he realize how abundant, happy, and beautiful his life in the Garden of Eden had been, and give thanks to God in his true heart.

His descendants also came to distinguish light from darkness, spirit from flesh, and good from evil through the human cultivation while experiencing many kinds of hardships. Therefore, once we receive salvation and go to heaven, the light of the sun or the moon that were required for human cultivation would no longer be necessary.

Since God Himself stays in the City of New Jerusalem, there is no darkness at all. Moreover, the light of God's glory shines the most in New Jerusalem; quite naturally, the City does not require the sun or the moon, or any lamps or lights to shine on it.

The Lamb who is the lamp of New Jerusalem

John could not find anything that gave out light like the sun or the moon, or any kind of light bulbs. This is because Jesus Christ, who is the Lamb, becomes the lamp in the City of New Jerusalem.

Since the first man Adam committed the sin of disobedience, the human race had to fall to the way of death (Romans 6:23). The God of love sent Jesus to this earth to resolve this problem of sin. Jesus, the Son of God who came in flesh to this earth, cleansed our sins by shedding His blood, and became the first fruit of resurrection by breaking the power of death.

As a result, all those who accept Jesus as their personal Savior receive life and can partake in the resurrection, enjoy eternal life in heaven, and receive answers to whatever they ask on this earth. Furthermore, God's children can now become the light of the world by living in the light themselves, and give glory to God through Jesus Christ. In other words, the way a lamp can give out light, the light of God's glory shines more brightly through the Savior Jesus.

The Rapture of New Jerusalem

When we look into the City of New Jerusalem from afar, we can see beautiful buildings made of so many kinds of precious stones and gold through the clouds of glory. The entire City seems to be alive with the mixture of many kinds of light: the lights coming out from the houses made of precious stones; the light of God's glory; and the lights coming out from the walls made of jasper and pure gold in clear and bluish colors.

How can we possibly express in word the emotion and excitement of entering New Jerusalem? The City is so beautiful, magnificent, and ecstatic beyond our imagination. In the center of the City is God's throne, the origin of the River of the Water of Life. Around God's throne are houses of Elijah, Enoch, Abraham, and Moses, Mary Magdalene, and the Virgin Mary, all of whom were loved by God very, very much.

The castle of the Lord

The castle of the Lord is located on the right and downward of God's throne, where God stays for worship services or banquets in the City of New Jerusalem. In the Lord's castle, there is a huge building with golden roof at the center, and around it are spread so many kinds of buildings endlessly. Especially, there are many crosses of glory, surrounded by brilliant lights, over the golden, dome-shaped roofs. They remind us of the fact that we received salvation and arrived at heaven because Jesus had taken the cross.

The big building in the center is a cylinder-shaped structure, but since it is adorned with many delicately-crafted jewels, beautiful lights shine from each jewel to mix up to make rainbow colors. If we were to compare the Lord's castle to any man-made buildings on the earth, it bears the closest resemblance to the St. Basil's Cathedral in Moscow, Russia. However, the style, materials, and size cannot possibly be compared to the most magnificent building ever designed or built on this earth.

Other than this building at the center, there are many buildings in the castle of the Lord. God the Father Himself provided these buildings so that those who have close relationship in spirit could stay with their loved ones. Facing the castle of the Lord, the houses of the twelve disciples are lined up. On the front are the houses of Peter, John, and James, and other disciples' houses stand behind them. What is special is that there are places for Mary Magdalene and the Virgin Mary to stay in the castle of the Lord. Of course, these places are for the two women to stay temporarily when they are invited by the Lord, and their actual castle-like dwelling places are located close to God's throne.

The castle of the Holy Spirit

On the left and downward of God's throne is the castle of the Holy Spirit. This gigantic castle represents meek and soft, mother-like characteristics of the Holy Spirit with many harmonious dome-shaped buildings of varying sizes.

The roof of the biggest building at the center of the castle is like one big piece of sardius, which represents passion. Around this building flows the River of the Water of Life that originates from the throne of God and the castle of the Lord.

All the castles in New Jerusalem are so enormous and magnificent beyond measure, but the castles of the Lord and the Holy Spirit are especially magnificent and beautiful. Their size is close to that of a city than a castle, and they are built in a very special style. This is because, unlike other houses that are built by angels, they are built by God the Father Himself. Moreover, like the castle of the Lord, the houses of those who united with the

Holy Spirit and accomplished God's kingdom in the era of the Holy Spirit, are built beautifully around the castle of the Holy Spirit.

The Grand Sanctuary

There are many buildings under construction around the castle of the Holy Spirit, and there is especially a magnificent and great building. It has a round roof and twelve tall pillars, and there are twelve big gates between the pillars. This is the Grand Sanctuary made after the City of New Jerusalem.

However, John in Revelation 21:22 says, *"I saw no temple in it, for the Lord God the Almighty and the Lamb are its temple."* Why could John not see a temple? People usually think that God needs a place to stay, i.e. in a temple the way we need a dwelling place. Therefore, on this earth, we worship Him in sanctuaries where God's Word is preached.

As declared in John 1:1, *"In the beginning was the Word, and the Word was with God, and the Word was God,"* where the Word is, there is God; wherever the Word is preached is the sanctuary. However, God Himself stays in the City of New Jerusalem. God, who is the Word itself, and the Lord who is one with God, dwell in the City of New Jerusalem, so no other temple is necessary. Thus, through the apostle John, God let us know that no temple is necessary and that God and the Lord are the temple in New Jerusalem.

Then, we are left to wonder, why is a Grand Sanctuary that was not present during the apostle John's time, being built today? As we find in Acts 17:24, *"The God who made the world and all things in it, since He is Lord of heaven and earth, does not dwell in temples made with hands,"* God does not dwell in a particular temple building.

Likewise, although God's throne is in heaven, He still wants to build the Grand Sanctuary that represents His glory; the Grand Sanctuary becomes solid evidence in displaying God's power and glory all over the world.

Today, there are many great and magnificent buildings on this earth. People invest huge sums of money and build beautiful structures for their own glory and according to their own desire, but no one is doing the same for God, who is truly worthy of glorification. Therefore, God wants to build the beautiful and magnificent Grand Sanctuary through His children who have received the Holy Spirit and become sanctified. He, then, wants to be properly glorified by people of all nations with this (1 Chronicles 22:6-16).

Similarly, when the beautiful Grand Sanctuary is built the way God wants, all people from all nations will glorify God and prepare themselves as brides of the Lord to receive Him. That is why God prepared the Grand Sanctuary as a center of evangelization to lead countless people to the way of salvation, and lead them to New Jerusalem at the end of the time. If we realize this providence of God, build the Grand Sanctuary, and give glory to God, He will reward us according to our deeds and build the same Grand Sanctuary in the City of New Jerusalem.

Thus, when looking at the Grand Sanctuary made of jewels and gold that cannot be compared to any earthly materials, those who enter heaven will be perpetually grateful for God's love that led us to the way of glory and blessing through the human cultivation.

Heavenly houses decorated with jewels and gold

Around the castle of the Holy Spirit are houses decorated with many kinds of precious stones, and there are also many houses still under construction. We can see many angels at work, placing beautiful jewels here and there or clearing the site of the houses. In this way, God gives rewards according to each individual's deeds and puts them in his or her house.

God once showed me houses of two very faithful workers of this church. One of them has been a source of great strength to the church by praying day and night for the kingdom of God, and her house is built with the aroma of prayer and perseverance, and it is decorated from the entrance with brilliant jewels.

Also, to accommodate her sweet characteristics, there is a table at one corner of the garden at which she can have tea time with her loved ones. There are many kinds of small flowers of different colors on the grass of the plain. This describes only the entrance and the garden of the person's house. Can you imagine how much more magnificent the main building would be?

The other house God showed me belogns to a worker who has devoted herself in literary evangelization on this earth. I could see one room among many in the main building. There are a desk, a chair, and a candlestick, all of which are made of gold, and many books in this room. This is to reward and in remembrance of her work of glorifying God through literary evangelization, and because God knows she enjoys reading very much.

Likewise, God does not only prepare our heavenly houses but also gives us such beautiful items we cannot imagine in order to reward us for having given up and abandoned our worldly pleasure on this earth to devote ourselves fully in accomplishing God's kingdom.

Forever Abiding with the Lord Our Groom

In the City of New Jerusalem, many kinds of banquets, including the one held by God the Father, are continuously held. This is because those who live in New Jerusalem can invite brothers and sisters living in other dwelling places of heaven.

How glorious and happy it would be if you could live in New Jerusalem and be invited by the Lord to share love with Him and attend pleasant banquets!

Warm welcome at the Lord's castle

When people in New Jerusalem are invited by the Lord their groom, they adorn themselves as the most beautiful brides and with joyful hearts gather at the Lord's castle. When these brides of the Lord arrive at His castle, two angels on each side of the shiny main gate politely welcome them. At this time, the fragrance from the walls decorated with many jewels and flowers surround their bodies to add to their joy.

Upon entering the main gate, the sound of praise that touches the deepest side of the spirit is faintly heard. Then, upon hearing this sound, peace, happiness, and gratitude for God's love overflow their hearts because they know He has led them there.

While they are walking on the golden road clear as glass to reach the main building, they are escorted by angels and pass many beautiful buildings and gardens. Until reaching the main building, their hearts throb in hopes of meeting the Lord. Approaching closer to the main building, they can now see the Lord Himself waiting to receive them. Tears block their sight but they run to the Lord in earnest desire to see Him even a second sooner. The Lord waits for them with His arms wide open, and with His face full of love and meekness, He hugs each of them.

The Lord tells them, "Come, My beautiful brides! You are most welcome!" The ones who are invited confess their love in His bosom, saying, "I am thankful from the bottom of my heart for your inviting me!" Then, they walk here and there hand in hand with the Lord like couples deeply in love and, have lovely conversations they longed to have since their time on this earth. To the right of the main building is a big lake, and the Lord explains in detail His feelings and circumstances of the time of His ministry on the earth.

By the lake remindful of the Sea of Galilee

Why does this lake remind them of the Sea of Galilee? God made this lake in remembrance because the Lord began and did much of His ministry around the Sea of Galilee (Matthew 4:23). Isaiah 9:1 reads, *"But there will be no more gloom for her who was in anguish; in earlier times He treated the land of Zebulun and the land of Naphtali with contempt, but later on He shall make it glorious, by the way of the sea, on the other side of Jordan, Galilee of the Gentiles."* It was prophesied that the Lord would begin His ministry at the Sea of Galilee and the prophecy was fulfilled.

Many fish that give out different colors of lights swim in this big lake. In John 21, the resurrected Lord appeared to Peter, who had not caught any fish, and told him, *"Cast the net on the right-hand side of the boat and you will find a catch"* (v. 6), and when Peter complied, he caught 153 fish. In the lake in the castle of the Lord are also 153 fish, and this is also in remembrance of the Lord's ministry. When these fish jump up to the air and do adorable tricks, their colors change in many ways to add to the joy and pleasure of the invited.

The Lord walks on this lake just as He did on the Sea of Galilee on this earth. Then, those who are invited would stand around the lake in gladness and long to hear the Lord speak. He explains in detail the situation when He walked on the Sea of Galilee on this earth. Then, Peter, who could walk on the water for a moment on this earth by obeying the Word of the Lord, would feel sorry for that he sank into water because of little faith (Matthew 14:28-32).

A museum honoring the Lord's ministry

Visiting various sites with the Lord, people now think of the times of their cultivation on this earth, and are overwhelmed by the love of the Father and the Lord who prepared heaven. They arrive at a museum on the left of the main building in the Lord's castle. God the Father Himself built it in remembrance of the Lord's ministry on the earth so that people can see and feel it like reality. For example, the place where Jesus was judged by Pontius Pilate and the Via Dolorosa where He carried the cross up to Golgotha are rebuilt the same way. When people see these places, the Lord explains the situations at that time in detail.

A little while ago, in the inspiration of the Holy Spirit, I came to learn what the Lord confessed at that time, and I would like to share some of it with you. It is a heartfelt confession of the Lord, who came to this earth after forsaking all the glory in heaven, that He made while He was walking up to Golgotha with the cross.

Father! My Father!
My Father, who is perfect in the light,
You truly love everything!

The land I stepped on
for the first time with You,
and the people,
since they were created,
have now corrupted so much…

Now I realize
why You have sent Me here,
why You let Me suffer these hardships
coming from the corrupted hearts of people,
and why You let Me come down here
from the glorious place in heaven!
Now I can feel and realize
all these things
in the depths of My heart.

But Father!
I know that You will restore everything
in Your justice and hidden secrets.
Father!
All these things are momentary.
But because of the glory
You will give Me,
and the ways of light
that You open for these people,
Father,
I take this cross with hope and joy.

Father, I am able to go this way
because I believe
You will open this way and light

with Your permission and in Your love,
and You will shine Your Son
with the beautiful lights
when all these things are over
in a short while.

Father!
The land I used to step on is made of gold,
the roads I used to walk is also gold,
the scents of the flowers I used to smell
cannot be compared to
the ones on this earth,
the materials of the clothes
I used to wear
are so different from these,
and the place I used to live is
such a glorious place.
And I would like these people
to know this beautiful and peaceful place.

Father,
I realize every bit of Your providence.
Why You gave birth to Me,
why You gave Me this duty,
and why You let Me come down here
to step on the corrupted land,
and to read the minds of the corrupted people.
I praise You Father
for Your love, greatness,
and all these things that are flawless.

My dear Father!
People think that I do not defend Myself,
that I claim to be the king of the Jews.
But Father,
how can they grasp the memories
flowing from My heart,
the love for the Father flowing from My heart,
the love for these people
flowing from My heart?

Father,
many people will realize and understand
the things that are to take place later
through the Holy Spirit
You will give them as a gift
after I am gone.
Because of this momentary pain,
Father, do not shed tears
and do not turn Your face from Me.
Do not let Your heart be filled with pain,
Father!

Father, I love You!
Until I get crucified,
shed My blood and breathe My last,
Father, I think of all the things
and the heart of these people.

Father, do not feel sorry
but be glorified through Your Son,
and the providence and all the plans of the Father

will be wholly completed forever and more.

The Lord Jesus explains what was going through His mind while on the cross: the glory of heaven; Himself standing before the Father; the people; the reason why the Father had to give Him that duty, and so on.

Those who are invited to the castle of the Lord shed tears as they listen to this and give thanks to the Lord in tears for having taken the cross on their behalf, and confess from the depths of their hearts, "My Lord, You are my true Savior!"

In remembrance of the Lord's hardships, God made many roads of jewels in the castle of the Lord. When someone walks on the roads built and adorned with many jewels of many colors, the lights become brighter and it feels like walking on water. Furthermore, in remembrance of being hung on the cross to redeem human beings from their sins, there God the Father made a wooden cross with blood smeared on it. There is also the stable of Bethlehem in which the Lord was born, and there are many things to see and feel the Lord's ministry like reality. When people visit these sites, they can vividly see and hear about the Lord's work so that they can feel the love of the Lord and the Father in greater depth and give glory and thanks forever more.

The Glory of New Jerusalem Residents

New Jerusalem is the most beautiful place in heaven rewarded to those who accomplished sanctification in their hearts and were faithful in all God's house. Revelation 21:24-26 tell us what kinds of people receive the glory of entering New Jerusalem:

The nations will walk by its light, and the kings of the earth will bring their glory into it. In the daytime (for there will be no night there) its gates will never be closed; and they will bring the glory and the honor of the nations into it.

The nations walk by its light

Here, "nations" refers to all the people who are saved regardless of their ethnic backgrounds. Although people's citizenships, races, and other attributes differ from one person to another, once they are saved through Jesus Christ, they all become God's children with the citizenships of the heavenly kingdom.

Therefore, the phrase "nations will walk by its light" means that all of God's children will walk within the light of God's glory. However, not all the children of God will have the glory to freely come into the City of New Jerusalem. This is because those who stay in Paradise, the First, Second, or Third Kingdom of Heaven can go inside New Jerusalem on an invitation-only basis. Only those who were completely sanctified and were faithful in all God's house can have the honor to see God the Father face to face in New Jerusalem forever.

The kings of the earth will bring their glory

The phrase "the kings of the earth" refers to the ones who used to be spiritual leaders on this earth. They shine like the twelve jewels of the twelve foundations of the walls of New Jerusalem and have the qualifications to perpetually dwell in the City. Similarly, those who are recognized by God, when they stand before Him, will bring with them offerings they have prepared with their whole hearts. By "offerings" I mean everything with which they gave glory to God with their hearts that are as pure and clear as crystal.

Therefore, "the kings of the earth will bring their glory into it" means that they will prepare as offerings all the things that they have arduously worked for God's kingdom and given glory to Him, and enter New Jerusalem with them.

Kings of this earth give offerings to kings of greater and stronger nations as a means to flatter them, but the offering to God is given with the gratitude for having led them to the way of salvation and eternal life. God receives this offering gladly and rewards them with the honor to stay forever in the City of New Jerusalem.

In New Jerusalem, there is no darkness because God, who Himself is the light, stays there. Since there is no night, evil, death, or thief, it is not necessary to close the gates of New Jerusalem. Yet, the reason why the Scriptures says "daytime" is because we have only limited knowledge and capacity to fully understand heaven.

Bringing the glory and the honor of the nations

Then, what does the phrase "they will bring the glory and the honor of the nations into it" mean? "They" here refers to all those who have received salvation from all nations of the earth, and "they will bring the glory and the honor of the nations into it" means that these people will come into New Jerusalem with the things with which they gave glory to God, while giving out the scent of Jesus Christ on this earth.

When a child studies hard and his grades go up, he will boast to his parents. The parents will be joyful with him because they will be proud of their child's hard work, even if he may not have gotten the best marks. In the same way, to the extent we act with faith for the kingdom of God on this earth, we give out the scent of Jesus Christ and give glory to God, and He receives this with joy.

It is mentioned above that "the kings of the earth will bring their glory into it," and the reason why it reads "kings of the earth" first is to show the spiritual order or rank in which people come before God.

Those who are qualified to stay in New Jerusalem forever with the glory like the sun will go before God first, followed by then those who are saved from all nations with respective glory. We must realize that if we do not have qualifications to live in New Jerusalem forever, we can visit the City only occasionally.

Those who can never enter New Jerusalem

The God of love wants everybody to receive salvation and reward each one with a dwelling place and heavenly prizes according to his or her deeds. That is why those who do not have the qualifications to enter New Jerusalem will enter the Third, Second, or First Kingdom of Heaven, or Paradise according to the measure of their faith. God holds special banquets and invites them to New Jerusalem so that they too may enjoy the magnificence of the City.

However, you can see that there are some people who can never enter New Jerusalem even if God wants to have mercy on them. Namely, those who did not receive salvation can never see the glory of New Jerusalem.

> *Nothing unclean, and no one who practices abomination and lying, shall ever come into it, but only those whose names are written in the Lamb's book of life (Revelation 21:27).*

"Unclean" here refers to judging and condemning others, and complaining seeking one's own interests and benefits. This kind of person assumes the role of a judge and condemns others at his own will, instead of understanding them. "Abomination" here refers to all the deeds coming from the abominable heart in a double-minded way. Since such people have capricious and fickle hearts and minds, they give thanks only when they receive the answers to their prayers, but soon complain and lament if they face trials. Similarly, the ones with shameful hearts deceive their conscience and do not hesitate to change their minds in pursuit of their own interests.

A "lying" person is one who cheats himself and his conscience, and we have to know that this kind of deceit becomes a trap of Satan. There are some liars who lie habitually and some others who tell a lie for the good of others, but God wants us to throw away even this kind of lies. There are some people who do harm to others by giving a false testimony, and this kind of person who cheats others with an evil intent will not be saved. Furthermore, those who cheat the Holy Spirit or in God's works are also deemed "lying." Judas Iscariot, one of the twelve disciples of Jesus, was in charge of the money bag and kept on cheating in God's work by stealing from the treasury, and committing other sins. When Satan finally entered him, he sold Jesus for thirty pieces of silver and was eternally discarded.

There are some people who see the sick people healed and demons driven out by the Holy Spirit in the power of God, but still deny these works and instead say they are the works of Satan. These people cannot enter heaven because they blaspheme and speak against the Holy Spirit. We should not tell a lie in any circumstances in the sight of God.

Those whose names are erased from the Book of Life

When we are saved by faith, our names are recorded in the Book of Life of the Lamb (Revelation 3:5). Yet, this does not mean that everybody who has accepted Jesus Christ will be saved. We can actually be saved only when we act according to God's Word and resemble the heart of the Lord by circumcising our hearts. If we still act in untruth even after accepting Jesus Christ, our names will be erased from the Book of Life and in the end not even receive salvation.

On this, Revelation 22:14-15 tells us that blessed are those who wash their robes and those who do not wash their robes will not be saved:

> *Blessed are those who wash their robes, so that they may have the right to the tree of life, and may enter by the gates into the city. Outside are the dogs and the sorcerers and the immoral persons and the murderers and the idolaters, and everyone who loves and practices lying.*

"Dogs" here refers to the ones who do the untruth again and again. Those who do not turn away from their evil acts but keep on repeating evil can never be saved. They are like a dog going back to its vomit and a sow, just after washed, going back to her wallowing in the mud. This is because they seem to have thrown away their evil, but repeat their ways of evilness, and they seem to have become better, but return to evil.

However, God recognizes the faith of those who strive to act good even if they cannot act wholly according to God's word yet. They will eventually be saved because they are still changing and God deems their effort faith.

"Sorcerers" refer to "those who practice magic arts." They act abominably, and make others worship false gods. This is very, very abominable to God.

"Immoral persons" commits adultery even if he/she has a wife or a husband. There is not only physical adultery but also spiritual adultery, which is to love anything more than God. If a person who vividly experienced the living God and realized His love still turns to love other worldly things such as money or his family more than he loves God, the person commits spiritual adultery and it is not right before God.

"Murderers" commit physical or spiritual murders. If you know the spiritual meaning of "murder," you probably would not be able to boldly say that you have not murdered anybody. A spiritual murder is to cause God's children to sin and lose their spiritual life (Matthew 18:7). If you cause any pain to others with anything that is against the truth, it is also spiritual murder (Matthew 5:21-22).

Also, it is all spiritual murder to hate, envy and be jealous, judge, condemn, argue, get angry, cheat, lie, have dissension and faction, slander, and be without love and mercy (Galatians 5:19-21). Sometimes, however, there are some people who lose their footing in their own evil. For example, if they leave God because they are disappointed by somebody in the church, it is in their own evil. If they had truly believed in God, they would never have lost their footing.

Also, "idolaters" is one of the things God hates the most.

In idol-worshipping, there are physical idol-worshipping and spiritual idol-worshipping. Physical idol-worshipping is making a formless god as an image and worshipping it (Isaiah 46:6-7). Spiritual idol-worshipping is anything that you love more than God. If one loves his or her spouse or children more than he/she loves God in pursuit of their own desire, or breaks God's commandments by loving money, fame, or knowledge more than he/she loves God, this is spiritual idol-worshipping.

These kinds of people, no matter how much they may call out "Lord, Lord" and attend church, cannot be saved and enter heaven because they do not love God.

Therefore, if you accepted Jesus Christ, received the Holy Spirit as God's gift, and your name is recorded in the Book of Life of the Lamb, please keep in mind that you can enter heaven and advance to New Jerusalem only when you act according to God's Word.

New Jerusalem is the place where only those who are completely sanctified in their hearts and faithful in all God's house can enter.

On the one hand, those who enter New Jerusalem can meet God face to face, have lovely talks with the Lord, and take pleasure in unimaginable honor and glory. On the other hand, those who stay in Paradise, the First, Second, or Third Kingdom of Heaven can visit the City of New Jerusalem only when they are invited to special banquets including the ones held by God the Father.

Chapter 8

"I Saw the Holy City, New Jerusalem"

"Blessed are you when people insult you and persecute you,
and falsely say all kinds of evil against
you because of Me. Rejoice and be glad,
for your reward in heaven is great;
for in the same way they persecuted the prophets
who were before you."

- Matthew 5:11-12

In the City of New Jerusalem, heavenly houses are being built so that people whose hearts wholly resemble God's heart will live in them later. According to each owner's taste, they are being built by archangels and angels in charge of construction, with the Lord as supervisor. This is a privilege only those who enter New Jerusalem can enjoy. Sometimes, God Himself gives an order to an archangel to build a house specifically for a certain person so that it can be made exactly according to the owner's tastes. He does not forget even one drop of tear that His children shed for His kingdom and rewards them with beautiful and precious stones.

As we find in Matthew 11:12, God clearly tells us that to the extent to which we win in spiritual battles and mature in faith, we can possess a more beautiful place in heaven:

> *From the days of John the Baptist until now the kingdom of heaven suffers violence, and violent men take it by force.*

The God of love, for many years, has been leading us to advance to heaven forcefully, showing the heavenly houses of New Jerusalem clearly. This is because it is very near for the Lord, who went to prepare a place for us, to come back.

Heavenly Houses of Unimaginable Sizes

In New Jerusalem, there are many beautiful houses of unimaginable sizes. Among them, there is one beautiful and magnificent house built on a large area. At the center is a round, grand and beautiful three-story castle, and around the castle are many buildings and things to enjoy or kinds of rides found in an amusement park to make this place look like a world-famous tourist attraction. What is really surprising is that this city-like heavenly house belongs to an individual cultivated on this earth!

Blessed are the gentle, for they will inherit the earth

If we had financial capability on this earth, we can buy a large piece of land and build a beautiful house the way we want. Yet, in heaven, we cannot either buy any land or build any house regardless of the wealth we have, because God rewards us the land or houses according to our deeds.

Matthew 5:5 says, *"Blessed are the gentle, for they shall*

inherit the earth." Depending on the extent to which we resemble the Lord and accomplish spiritual meekness on this earth, we can "inherit the earth" in heaven. This is because one who is spiritually meek can embrace all people, and they can come to him and find rest and comfort. He would be in peace with everybody in any situations since his heart is soft and gentle as fluff.

Yet, if we compromise with the world and go against the truth in order to be at peace with other people, this is not at all spiritual meekness. One who is truly meek can not only embrace many people with a soft and warm heart, but also be brave and strong enough to risk even his life for the truth.

This kind of person can win many people's hearts and lead them to the way of salvation and to a better place in heaven because he has love and gentleness. That is why he can possess a grand house in heaven. Therefore, the house described below belongs to a truly meek person.

A city-like house

At the center of this house is a big castle decorated with many jewels and gold. Its roof is made with a round-shaped sardius and shines very brightly. Around the shiny, bright castle flows the River of the Water of Life that originates from the throne of God, and many buildings make this look like a metropolis. Also, there are amusement-park rides decorated with gold and many jewels.

On one side of the spacious land are forests, plain, and a big lake, and on the other side are vast hills with many kinds of flowers and waterfalls. Also, there is a sea on which a huge cruise ship like the Titanic is afloat and sailing around.

Now, let us take a tour of this splendid house. There are twelve gates on four sides, and let us go through the main gate from which we can see the main castle at the center.

This main gate is decorated with many jewels and guarded by two angels. They are masculine and look very strong. They stand without blinking their eyes, and their apparent dignity makes them appear very unapproachable.

On either side of the gate stand round and beautiful, big pillars. The walls decorated with many jewels and flowers seem endless. Entering the gate that opens automatically led by angels, you can see afar the big castle with a red roof that shines beautiful lights down on you.

Also, looking at many houses of different sizes decorated with many jewels, you cannot help yourself from being deeply moved by the love of God who rewards you thirty, sixty, or one hundred times of what you have done and offered. You are thankful for His having given His one and only Son to lead you to the way of salvation and eternal life. On top of this, He has also prepared for you such beautiful heavenly houses, and your heart will overflow with gratitude and joy.

Also, because a mild, clear and beautiful sound of praise can be heard all around the castle, inexpressible peace and happiness overwhelms your spirit and you will be full of emotion:

Far away in the depths of my spirit tonight
Rolls a melody sweeter than psalm;
In celestial like strains it unceasingly falls
O'er my soul like an infinite calm.
Peace! Peace! Wonderful peace
Coming down from the Father above!
Sweep over my spirit for ever, I pray,

In fathomless billows of love.

Golden roads as clear as glass

Now, let us go to the big castle at the center, walking along the golden road. Entering the main entrance, trees of gold and jewels with appetizing jewel fruit welcome the visitors on either side of the road. The visitors would then take a fruit. The fruit melts in the mouth and is so delicious that the whole body becomes energized and joyful.

On each side of the golden roads, flowers of many colors and sizes welcome and greet visitors with their scents. Behind them are golden turf and many kinds of trees that complement a beautiful garden. Flowers of beautiful rainbow colors look like they are giving out lights, and each flower gives out its unique scent. On some of these flowers, insects like butterflies of rainbow colors sit and chat with one another. On the trees are hanging many appetizing fruit among their shiny branches and leaves. Many kinds of birds with golden color feathers sit on the trees and sing to make the scene so peaceful and happy. There are also some animals roaming about peacefully.

A cloud automobile and a golden wagon

Now you are standing at the second gate. The house is so big that there is another gate inside the main gate. Before your eyes is a wide area that resembles a garage in which many cloud automobiles and a golden wagon are parked and you are overwhelmed by this incredulous scene.

The golden wagon, decorated with big diamonds and jewels, is for the owner of this house and seats one. When the wagon moves, it shines like a shooting star because of so many glittering jewels, and its speed is a lot faster than the cloud automobile.

A cloud automobile is surrounded by pure white clouds and beautiful lights of many colors, and has four wheels and wings. The vehicle runs on its wheels on the ground, and when it flies, the wheels automatically retract and the wings stretch out so that it can run and fly freely.

How great the authority and honor would it be to travel many places of heaven with the Lord in cloud automobiles, escorted by heavenly host and angels? If a cloud automobile is given to each person who enters New Jerusalem, can you imagine how much the owner of this house has been rewarded since there are *numerous* cloud automobiles in his garage?

A big castle at the center

When you arrive at the grand and beautiful castle in a cloud automobile, you can see a three-story building with sardius roof. This building is so enormous that it cannot be compared to any building on this earth. It appears that the whole castle is slowly revolving, giving out brilliant lights, and such bright lights make the castle look like it is alive. Pure gold and jasper brilliantly give out clear and transparent golden lights in bluish color. Yet, you cannot see through, and it looks like a sculpture without any joints. The walls and flowers around these walls give out beautiful scents to add to happiness and joy that cannot be described with words. Flowers of different sizes make the grand scenery, and their different shapes and scents make an excellent combination.

What, then, is the specific reason that God has provided such a vast piece of land and a grand, beautiful house? This is because God never misses or forgets anything that His children worked

for His kingdom and righteousness on this earth and rewards
them abundantly.

I rejoice again and again
in My beloved one.
This one loved Me so much
that he gave his everything.
He loved Me more than
his parents and brothers,
He did not spare his own children,
and he considered his life worthless
and gave it up for Me.

His eyes were always focused on Me.
He listened to My Word fully.
He only sought My glory.
He was only thankful
even when he was under unjust suffering.
Even in the midst of persecutions,
in love he prayed for
those who persecuted him.
He never forsook anybody
even though he betrayed him.
He performed his duty with joy
even when he had unbearable sorrows.
And he saved many souls
and fully accomplished My will,
bearing My heart.

Because he accomplished My will
and loved Me so much,

I have prepared for
this grand and splendid house
in New Jerusalem.

A Magnificent Castle with Complete Privacy

As you can see, there are God's touches especially in the houses of those who are greatly loved by Him. So those houses have different levels of beauty and light of glory than other houses even within New Jerusalem.

A big castle at the center is a place where the owner can enjoy complete privacy. It is to compensate his works and his prayers in tears in accomplishing God's kingdom and the fact that he looked after the souls day and night without any private life to enjoy.

The general structure of his castle has the main house at the center of the castle, and the castle has two layers of walls. There is an additional wall in the middle part between the main house at the center and the outer wall. So, the whole castle is divided into the inner castle and the outer castle, which are from the main house to the center wall and from the center wall to the outer wall respectively.

Therefore, to reach the main house of this castle, we have to pass the main gate and then another gate once again at the middle wall. On the outer wall are many gates, and the gate that is in line with the front of the main house is the main gate. The main gate is decorated with various gemstones and two angels guard it. The two angels have masculine faces and they look very strong. They don't even move their eyes while on guard, and we can feel the dignity from them.

On either side of the main gate are big cylindrical pillars. The walls are decorated with jewels and flowers, and they are so long that the end cannot be seen. As guided by the angels we enter into the main gate that opens automatically, brilliant and beautiful lights shine on us. And there is a golden road that is like crystal that stretches out directly to the main gate.

As we walk the golden road, we will reach the second gate. This gate is located at the middle wall that separates the inner castle and the outer castle. As we pass this second gate, there is a place like a mega size parking lot on earth. Here, numerous cloud-like automobiles are parked. There is also the golden chariot among the cloud automobiles.

The main house of this castle is as big as to be bigger than any building on earth. It is a three-story building. Each floor of the building is cylindrical shape, and the area of each floor becomes smaller as you go up from floor to floor. The roof is like an onion-shaped dome.

The walls of the main house are made with pure gold and jasper. So, the bluish light and the clear and transparent golden light give out such magnificent lights in harmony. The light is so strong that it feels like the house itself is alive and moving. The whole building gives out brilliant lights and it looks like it is spinning slowly.

Now, let us enter this big castle!

Twelve gates to enter the main house of the castle

This main house has twelve gates to enter. Because the size of the main house is so big, the distance from one gate to another is quite far. The gates are arch-shaped, and each one has an engraving of a picture of a key. Below the picture of the key is inscribed the name of the gate in the heavenly alphabet. These letters are inscribed with jewels, and each gate is decorated with one kind of jewel respectively.

Below them are the explanations as to why each gate is named such. God the Father has condensed what the owner of this house has done on earth and expressed it on the twelve gates.

The first gate is the 'Gate of Salvation.' It has an explanation about how this owner became a shepherd of so many people and guided countless souls to salvation all around the world. Next to the Gate of Salvation is the 'Gate of New Jerusalem.' Below the name of the gate is the explanation that the owner guided so many souls into New Jerusalem.

Next, there is the 'Gates of Power.' First, there are four gates for the four levels of power, and then, there are the Gate of Power of Creation and the Gate of Most High Power of Creation. On these gates are explanations about how each kind of power healed so many people and glorified God.

The ninth is the 'Gate of Revelation,' and this gate has the explanation that the owner received so much revelation and explained the Bible very clearly. The tenth is the 'Gate of Achievements.' It is to commemorate the achievements like the construction of the Grand Sanctuary.

The eleventh is the 'Gate of Prayer.' This gate tells us about how this owner prayed with all his life to fulfill God's will with his love for God, and how he mourned and prayed for the souls.

The last and twelfth is a gate with the meaning of 'Winning against the enemy devil, Satan.' It has the explanation that the owner overcame everything with faith and love when the enemy devil, Satan tried to harm him and to put him into despair.

Special inscriptions and designs on the walls

The walls, made of pure gold and jasper, are full of designs with reverberating writings and drawings. Every detail about the persecutions and mockeries he faced for the kingdom of God, and all the deeds with which he glorified the Lord are recorded. What is more amazing is that God Himself engraved the writings in poem and the letters give out beautiful and brilliant lights.

If you enter the castle after passing one of these gates, you see objects that are much more beautiful than what you had seen outside. The lights from jewels overlap two or three times to make it appear so gorgeous.

Inscriptions about the owner's tears, endeavors, and efforts on this earth are carved on the inner walls as well and they give out such brilliant lights. The times of his earnest overnight prayers for the kingdom of God and the pure aroma of giving up himself as a drink offering for the souls are recorded as a poem and give out beautiful lights.

Yet, God the Father has hidden most of the details of the inscriptions so that God Himself could show it to the owner when he arrives at this place. This is so that God may receive his heart that glorifies the Father with deep emotion and tears when He shows those writings to him, telling him, "I have prepared this for you."

Even in this world, when we love somebody, some people

repeatedly write the names of the person. They write the name on a note or in diaries, on the beach, or even carved on trees or hewn in rocks. They don't know how to express their love so they just keep on writing the name of the person they love.

In a similar way, there is a square shaped golden plate that has only three words. The three words are: 'Father', 'Lord', and 'Me.' The owner of the house couldn't just express his love for the Father and the Lord with words. It shows his heart this way.

Meetings and banquets on the first floor

This castle is not open to others most of the time, but is open on occasion when there are banquets or balls held here. There is a very big hall in which countless people can gather and have banquets. It is also used as a meeting place in which the owner shares love and joy, having conversations with the guests.

The hall is round and so big that you cannot see one end from the other. The floor is of some whitish color and very smooth. It has many jewels and shines brilliantly. In the middle of the hall is a three-level chandelier to add to the dignity of the room, and there are more golden chandeliers of different sizes on the sides of the walls to add to the beauty of the hall. Also, at the center of the hall is a round stage, and many tables are placed in many layers around the stage. Those who are invited take their seats in the order and have friendly conversations.

All the decorations inside the building are made according to the taste of the owner, and their lights and shapes are so beautiful and delicate. Each jewel in it has God's touch, and it is such an honor to be invited to this banquet held by the owner of this house.

Secret rooms and reception rooms on the second floor

On the second floor of this big castle, there are many rooms and each room has a secret, fully revealed only in heaven, which God rewards according to the owner's deeds. A certain room has countless crowns of different kinds, like a museum of some sort. Many crowns including a golden crown, a gold-decoration crown, a crystal crown, a pearl crown, a flower-decoration crown, and many other crowns adorned with many kinds of jewels are neatly placed. These crowns are rewarded each time the owner accomplishes God's kingdom and gives glory to Him on this earth, and their sizes and shapes, and materials and decorations are all different to show the difference in honor. Also, there are big rooms that serve as closets for clothing and to safeguard jewel ornaments, and they are maintained with special care by angels.

There is also a neat square room without many decorations called "The Room of Prayer." It is given because the owner has offered up much prayer on this earth. Furthermore, there is a room with several television sets. This room is called "The Room of Agony and Mourning" and in here the owner can watch all the things of his earthly life whenever he wants. God has preserved every single moment and event of the owner's life because he suffered tremendously while doing God's work and ministry and shed many tears for the souls.

There is also a beautifully decorated place to receive prophets on the second floor, in which the owner can share his love and have friendly conversations with them. He can meet such prophets as Elijah who went up to heaven by a chariot and horses of fire, Enoch who walked with God for 300 years, Abraham who pleased God with faith, Moses who was more humble than anyone on the face of the earth, the ever-so passionate apostle

Paul, and the rest, and enjoy conversing with them about their lives and circumstances on the earth.

Third floor reserved to share love with the Lord

The third floor of the big castle is decorated so wondrously to receive the Lord and have lovely conversations as long and much as possible. This is given because the owner loved the Lord more than anyone else, and tried to resemble His deeds by reading the Four Gospels, and served and loved everybody the way the Lord had served His disciples. Moreover, he prayed with so many tears to lead countless souls to the way of salvation by receiving God's power as the Lord did and actually displayed innumerable evidences of the living God. Tears poured down whenever he thought of the Lord, and many nights he could not sleep because he earnestly missed the Lord. Also, like the Lord who prayed all night, the owner prayed all night so many times and tried his best to wholly accomplish God's kingdom.

How joyful and happy he would be when he can meet the Lord face to face and share his love with Him in New Jerusalem!

I can see my Lord!
I can place the light of His eyes
in my own,
I can put His mild smile in my heart,
and all this is such great joy to me.

My Lord,
how much I love You!
You have seen everything
and You know everything.

Now I take great joy
in being able to confess my love.
I love You, Lord.
I missed You so much.

Conversations with the Lord will never grow boring or tiresome.

God the Father, who received this love, decorated the interior, the ornaments, and jewels so beautifully on the third floor of this magnificent house. The elaborateness and splendor cannot be described, and the level of the lights is special. Likewise, you can feel the justice and delicate love of God who rewards you according to your deeds just by looking around the houses of heaven.

Sightseeing Spots of Heaven

What else is there around the big castle? If I try to describe this city-like house to the minutest detail, it will be more than enough to write a book. Around the castle are a big garden and many kinds of buildings that are beautifully decorated standing in harmony. Such facilities as a swimming pool, an amusement park, cottages, and an opera house make this house look like a major tourist attraction.

God rewards everything according to one's deeds

The reason the owner can have this kind of house with so many facilities is because he devoted all his body, mind, time, and money to God on this earth. God rewards everything he did for the kingdom of God including leading countless souls to the way of salvation and building God's church. God is more than able to give us not only what we ask but also what we desire in our hearts. We see that God is able to design more perfectly and beautifully than any excellent architect or city planner on the earth, and show the unity and diversity at the same time.

On this earth, we can possess anything we want, most of the time, if we have enough money. In heaven, however, that is not the case. A house in which to live, clothes, jewels, crowns, or even the serving angels cannot be purchased or hired, but are given only according to the measure of one's faith and his faithfulness to God's kingdom.

As we find in Hebrews 8:5, *"[Those] who serve a copy and shadow of the heavenly things, just as Moses was warned by God when he was about to erect the tabernacle,"* this world is a shadow of heaven and most of the animals, plants, and the rest of the nature are found in heaven as well. They are much more beautiful than those of the earth.

Let us now explore the gardens filled with so many flowers and plants.

Worshipping places and the Grand Sanctuary

Down the castle at the center, there is a very big inner courtyard where many flowers and trees create such beautiful scenery. On either side of the castle are big worshipping places in which people can from time to time glorify God with praise. This heavenly house, which is unimaginably enormous, is like a famous tourist attraction equipped with so many facilities, and since it takes a long time for the people to look around the house, there are worshipping places in which they may rest.

Worship in heaven is totally different from the one to which we are used on this earth. We are not bound to formalities, but can give glory to God with new songs. If we sing of the glory of the Father and the love of the Lord, we will be refreshed as we receive the fullness of the Holy Spirit. Then we will have deeper emotions in our heart and we will be filled with thanks and joy.

In addition to these sanctuaries, this castle has a building that has exactly the same shape as a certain sanctuary that had existed on earth. While on earth, the owner of this castle had received the tasking from Father God to build an enormous and grand sanctuary, and the same kind of sanctuary is also built in New Jerusalem.

Much like David in the Old Testament, the owner of this castle also longed for God's Temple. There are many buildings in the world, but there isn't really any building that shows the dignity and glory of God. He always felt sorry for this fact.

He had such a great fervor to build a sanctuary that is only for God the Creator. God the Father accepted this longing heart and explained to him in great detail the shape, size, decorations, and even interior structures of the sanctuary. It was just impossible with human thoughts, but he acted only with faith, hope, and love; and finally, the Grand Sanctuary was constructed.

This Grand Sanctuary is not just a building that is huge and magnificent. It is the crystalloid of tears of the energy of those believers who truly love God. In order for this sanctuary to be built, the treasures of the world had to be utilized. The heart of the kings of nations had to be moved. And to do this, what was needed most were the powerful works of God that go beyond human imagination.

The owner of this castle overcame such difficult spiritual battles by himself to receive this kind of power. He believed in

God who makes impossible things possible with only goodness, love, and obedience. He prayed continually and as a result, he built the Grand Sanctuary that was joyfully accepted by God.

God the Father knowing all these facts, also built a reproduction of this Grand Sanctuary in the castle of this person. Of course, the Grand Sanctuary in heaven is built with gold and jewels that are more beautiful than materials on earth beyond comparison, though the shape is the same.

A performance hall like the Sydney Opera House

In this castle, there is a performance hall which looks similar to the Opera House of Sydney, Australia. There is a reason for God the Father to build such a performance hall in this castle. When the owner of this castle was on earth, he organized many performing teams understanding the heart of God who delights in praising. And he glorified God the Father greatly through beautiful and gracious Christian performing arts.

It wasn't just outward appearances, skills, and techniques. He guided the performers in a spiritual way so that they could praise God with true love from the depth of their hearts. He raised many performers who could offer up to God the kind of praises that God could really accept. For this God the Father has built a beautiful performing arts hall so that these performers will be able to freely demonstrate their skills to their heart's desire in this castle.

A big lake stretches out in front of this building, and it seems the building is floating on the water. When the water fountains shoot up the water from the lake, water droplets will fall giving out lights like jewels. The performance hall has a splendid stage decorated with many kinds of jewels and also many seats waiting for audiences. Here, angels will perform in beautiful costumes.

Those performing angels will dance in dresses emitting lights of shining jeweled transparency like wings of dragonflies. Each of their movements is perfectly flawless and beautiful. There are also angels that sing and play musical instruments. They play such beautiful and sweet melodies with sophisticated skills and technique.

But even though the skills of the angels are so good, the aroma from the praising and dancing is very different from that of God's children. God's children have deep love and thankfulness for God in their hearts. From the heart that was made beautiful through human cultivation comes out the aroma that can move the Father God.

Those children of God who have the duty of praising God on earth will have many chances to glorify God with their praises in heaven, too. If a praise leader goes into New Jerusalem, he/she can perform in this performing arts hall that looks like the Opera House. And the performances done in this place are sometimes live-broadcast to all dwelling places in the heavenly kingdom. Therefore, to stand on the stage of this hall just once will be such a great honor.

A cloud bridge of rainbow colors

The River of the Water of Life shining with silver lights flows all through the castle as it is surrounding the castle. It originates from God's throne and flows around the castles of the Lord and the Holy Spirit, New Jerusalem, the Third, Second, First Kingdoms of Heaven, Paradise, and returns to the throne of God.

People chat with the fish of so many beautiful colors while

sitting on gold and silver sands on either side of the River of the Water of Life. There are golden benches on each side of the River and around them are trees of life. Sitting on the golden benches and looking at the appetizing fruits, if you just think, 'Ah, those fruits look so delicious,' the serving angels will bring the fruit in a flower basket and politely hand them over to you.

There are also beautiful, arch-shaped cloud bridges around the River of the Water of Life. Walking on the cloud bridge with rainbow colors and overlooking the River that flows slowly beneath you, you feel so wonderful as if you were flying in the sky or walking on the water.

When you cross the River of the Water of Life, there is an outer courtyard with many kinds of flowers and a golden lawn, and here you feel something different from the way you felt in the inner courtyard.

An amusement park and a flower road

Crossing the cloud bridge, there is an amusement park that has many sorts of rides you have never seen, heard of, or imagined; even the best amusement parks of this world such as the Disneyland cannot be compared to this amusement park. Trains made of crystal run around the park, a pirate ship-themed ride made with gold and many jewels moves back and forth, a carrousel runs in a cheerful rhythm, and a big roller-coaster runs enthralling the riders. Whenever these rides decorated with many jewels move, they give out multiple-layered lights, and just being in there you are overwhelmed by the mood of the festival.

On one side of the outer courtyard, there is an endless flower road, and the whole road is covered with flowers so that you can walk on the flowers themselves. The heavenly body is so light that you cannot feel the weight, and the flowers are not trampled even if you walk on them. When you walk on the wide flower road smelling such soft scents of the flowers, the flowers close their petals as if they are shy and make a wave opening the petals widely. This is a special welcome and greeting. In fairy tales, flowers have their own faces and can have conversations, and it is the same in heaven.

You will be thoroughly elated to walk on the flowers and enjoy their scents, and the flowers feel happy and give their thanks to you for walking on them. When you step on them softly, they give out even more scents. Each flower has a different scent and the scents are mixed differently every time so that you can have new feelings every time you walk. The flower roads are spread here and there like a beautiful painting to add to the beauty of this heavenly house. Likewise, one person's house is enormous and seemingly boundless, and contains all kinds of facilities.

A big plain on which animals play peacefully

Over the flower roads is a big, wide plain and many kinds of animals that you could see on this earth are there as well. Of course, you can see many other animals in other places but there are almost all kinds of animals here, except for the ones that stood against God, such as dragons. The scenery before your eyes reminds you of the vast Savanna in Africa, and these animals do not leave their areas even though there is no fence and frolic freely. They are bigger than animals on this earth and have clearer colors shining more brightly. The law of the jungle does not apply to them here.

All animals are mild; even lions that are called the king of beasts are not aggressive at all but very mild and their golden furs are so lovely. Also, in heaven, you can talk freely with animals. Just imagine enjoying the beauty of the grand nature running on the wide plain riding lions or elephants. This is not something found only in a fairy tale but the privilege given to those who are saved and possess heaven

A private cottage and a golden chair for rest

Since this person's house is like a major tourist attraction in heaven for many to enjoy, God gave the owner a cottage especially for his private use. This cottage is placed on a small hill with a great view and has beautiful decorations. Not anyone can enter this cottage because it is for private use. The owner rests by himself in there or uses it to receive prophets such as Elijah, Enoch, Abraham, and Moses.

Also, there is another cottage made of crystal, and, unlike other buildings, it is so clear and transparent. Yet, you cannot see the inside from the outside and the entrance is off-limits. On the rooftop of this crystal cottage, there is a rotating golden chair. When the owner sits there, he can see the whole house at a glance beyond time and space. God has made it especially for the owner so that he could feel the joy looking at so many people visiting his house, or simply rest.

A hill of reminiscence and a road of contemplation

The road of contemplation, where trees of life are standing on each side, is so calm as if the time stopped. When the owner takes each step, peace comes out from the bottom of his heart and he is reminded of the things on this earth. If he thinks about the sun, the moon, and the stars, a round layer like a screen is put up above his head, and the sun, the moon, and the stars appear. In heaven the lights of the sun, the moon and the stars are not necessary because the entire place is surrounded by God's light of glory, but the layer is separately provided for him to think about the things on this earth.

Also, there is a place called the hill of reminiscence, and it forms a big village. This is where the owner can retrace his life on this earth, and its remnants are collected. The house in which he was born, schools he attended, towns and cities he lived in, the places where he faced trials, the place he met God for the first time, and the sanctuaries he built after becoming a minister are all made here in a chronological order.

Although the materials are obviously different from the ones of this earth, things on his earthly life are precisely replicated so that people can feel the traces of his earthly life vividly. How wondrous God's gentle and delicate love is!

Waterfalls and a sea with islands

As you keep on walking on the road of contemplation, you can hear a loud and clear sound from afar. It is the sound coming from the waterfall of so many colors. When the waterfall raises spray, beautiful jewels at the bottom of the waterfall shine such brilliant lights. This is such magnificent scenery to see a great flow of water fall three levels down from the top and flow into the River of the Water of Life. There are jewels that shine double or triple lights at both sides of the waterfall, and they give out such astonishing lights along with the spray of water. You can feel refreshed and energized just by looking at it.

There is also a pavilion on top of the waterfall on which

people can see the great sight or have a rest. You can see the heavenly house in its entirety, and the view is so grand and beautiful that it cannot be adequately described with the words of this earth.

There is a big sea behind the castle, and there are islands of different sizes in it. The spotless and clear seawater shines as if jewels were sprinkled on the water. It is also so beautiful to see the fish swim in the clear sea, and to one's surprise, beautiful houses of jade green color are built under the sea. On this earth, even the richest man cannot have a house under the sea.

However, since heaven is in the four-dimensional world in which everything is possible, there are countless things that we cannot understand or imagine to exist.

A gigantic cruise like the *Titanic* and a crystal boat

Islands on the sea have many kinds of wild flowers, singing birds, and precious stones to complement beautiful sceneries. Here, canoeing or surfing competitions are held to attract many heavenly citizens. There is a ship like the *Titanic* on the softly waving sea, and the vessel has many kinds of facilities such as swimming pools, theaters, and banquet halls on it. If you are on the transparent ship that is totally made of crystal, you feel like you are walking on the sea, and you can feel the beauty of the inside of the sea in a rugby ball-shaped submarine.

How happy it would be to be able to be on a ship like the *Titanic*, a crystal boat, or a rugby ball-shaped submarine in this beautiful place and spend even one day! Yet, since heaven is an eternal place, you can enjoy all these things forever only if you have the qualifications to enter New Jerusalem.

Many athletic, recreational facilities

There are also athletic and recreational facilities like golf courses, bowling alleys, swimming pools, tennis courts, volleyball courts, basketball courts, and so on. These are given as rewards because the owner could have enjoyed those sports on this earth but did not for the kingdom of God and spent all his time only for Him.

In the bowling alley, which is made of gold and jewels in a shape of a bowling pin, the ball and the pins are all made with gold and jewels. People play in groups of three to five, and they have a pleasant time together cheering one another. The ball does not feel like it weighs much, unlike the ones of the earth, so it will roll down the alley strongly even if you give it a gentle push. When it strikes the pins, brilliant lights along with a clear and beautiful sound come out.

On the golf course built on a golden lawn, the lawn lies down automatically for the ball to roll during the games. When the lawn lies down like dominoes, it looks like a golden wave. In New Jerusalem, even the lawn obeys the heart of its master. Furthermore, after putting, a piece of cloud comes next to the feet and moves its master to another course. How amazing and wondrous this is!

People have so much fun in the swimming pool as well. Since no one drowns in heaven, even those who could not swim on this earth can swim well naturally. Moreover, the water does not drench the clothes but rolls off like dew on a leaf. People can enjoy swimming any time because they can swim with the clothes on.

Lakes of many sizes and fountains in the gardens

There are many lakes of different sizes in the big, wide heavenly house. When fish of many colors in the lakes wave their fins as if they were dancing to please God's children, it looks like they are confessing their love aloud. You can also see fish changing their colors. A fish waving its silver color fins can suddenly change its color into pearl.

There are numerous gardens and each garden has a different name according to its unique beauty and characteristics. The beauty cannot be conveyed effectively because there is God's touch even on one leaf.

Fountains are also different according to the characteristics of each garden. Generally, fountains shoot up water, but there are fountains that give out many beautiful colors or scents. There are new and precious scents that you could not experience on this earth, such as the scent of endurance that you can feel from a pearl, the scent of endeavor and passion of sardius, the scent of self-sacrifice or faithfulness, and many more. At the center of the fountain that is being shot up, there are writings or drawings that explain the meanings of each fountain and why it has been created.

Furthermore, there are many other buildings and special spaces in that castle-like house, but it is such a pity that all those facilities cannot be explained in detail. What is important is that nothing is given without reason but everything is rewarded only according to how much one has worked for the kingdom and righteousness of God on this earth.

Great is your reward in heaven

By now you must have realized that this heavenly house is too enormous and great to imagine. The big castle with complete privacy is built at the center and there are many other buildings and facilities along with big gardens surrounding it; this house is like a tourist place of heaven. You probably cannot help yourself from getting so surprised since this house of unimaginable size is prepared by God for one person cultivated on this earth.

What, then, is the reason that God has prepared a heavenly house that is as big as a large city? Let us look at Matthew 5:11-12:

> *Blessed are you when people insult you and persecute you, and falsely say all kinds of evil against you because of Me. Rejoice and be glad, for your reward in heaven is great; for in the same way they persecuted the prophets who were before you.*

How much did the apostle Paul suffer in accomplishing God's kingdom? He suffered from unspeakable hardships and persecutions to preach Jesus the Savior to the Gentiles. We can see that he worked so hard for the kingdom of God from 2 Corinthians 11:23 onward. Paul was imprisoned, beaten, or in danger of death many times while he was preaching the gospel.

Yet, Paul never complained or grudged but rejoiced and was glad as the Word of God commanded him. After all, the door of the world mission for the Gentiles was opened through Paul. Therefore, he naturally entered New Jerusalem and came to possess the honor that shines like the sun in New Jerusalem.

God loves very much those who work arduously and are faithful even to sacrifice their lives, and blesses and rewards them with so many things in heaven.

The City of New Jerusalem is not reserved for any particular person, but anyone who sanctifies his heart to resemble God's own heart and fulfills his duty passionately can enter and live there.

I pray in the name of the Lord Jesus Christ that you may accomplish God's heart through fervent prayers and God's Word, and fulfill your duties completely so that you can enter New Jerusalem and confess to Him in tears, "I am so thankful for the great love of the Father."

Chapter 9

The First Banquet in New Jerusalem

"Whoever then annuls one of the least of
these commandments,
and teaches others to do the same,
shall be called least in the kingdom of heaven;
but whoever keeps and teaches them,
he shall be called great in the kingdom of heaven."
- Matthew 5:19

The holy City of New Jerusalem houses God's throne and, among countless people who are cultivated on this earth, those who have clear and beautiful hearts like crystal dwell there forever. Life in New Jerusalem with God the Trinity is full of unimaginable love, emotion, happiness, and joy. People enjoy an unending happiness attending worship services and banquets, and having affectionate conversations with one another.

If you attend a banquet in New Jerusalem held by God the Father Himself, you can watch performances and share love with an innumerable number of people from different dwelling places of heaven.

God the Trinity, who finished the human cultivation in long endurance, rejoices and feels happy looking at His beloved children.

The God of love has revealed to me in detail the life in New Jerusalem that is full of emotions beyond comprehension. The reason I could overcome evil with goodness and love the enemies even when I was suffering without any reason is because my heart is filled with hope for New Jerusalem.

Now, let us delve into how blessed it is to "accomplish God's heart" that is as clear and beautiful as crystal with a scene from the first banquet to be held in New Jerusalem as an example.

The First Banquet in New Jerusalem

Like on the earth, there are banquets in heaven, and through these we can understand the joy of heavenly life quite well. This is because they are the honorable places where we can see the richness and beauty of heaven at a glance and enjoy them. Just as people on this earth decorate themselves with the most beautiful things, and eat, drink and enjoy the best meals in a banquet held by a president of a country, when a banquet is held in heaven, it is filled with beautiful dancing and singing, and happiness.

A beautiful sound of praise from the hall

The banquet hall of New Jerusalem is so enormous and grand. If you pass the entrance and enter a room whose one end you cannot see from the other, a beautiful sound of heavenly music adds to the strong emotion already felt.

Wondrous is the light
that was since before the time began.
He shines everything

with that original light.
He gave birth to His Sons
and made the angels.

His glory is high
above heaven and earth
and is magnificent.
Beautiful is His grace
that He outstretched alone.
He outstretched His heart
and created the world.
Praise His great love with small lips.
Praise the Lord
who receives the praise and rejoices.
Lift His holy name
and praise Him forever.
His light is wondrous
and worthy to be praised.

The clear and elegant sound of music melts into the spirit to give excitement and such peace as a baby feels in the bosom of his mother.

The great gate of the banquet hall with the color of white gem is adorned with heavenly flowers of many shapes and colors and has a beautiful pattern engraved. You can see that God the Father has prepared even such a little thing to the minutest detail in His delicate love for His children at every corner of the City of New Jerusalem.

Passing the gate with the color of white gem

Countless people enter through the beautiful, big gate of the banquet hall in a line, and those who live in New Jerusalem enter first. They wear golden crowns that are taller than the crowns of other dwelling places and give out mild, beautiful lights. People wear white one-piece dresses that shine bright and brilliant lights. Its textile is as light and soft as silk, and it sways back and forth.

The dress, which is decorated with gold or many kinds of jewels, has shining embroideries of jewels on the neck and sleeves, and according to one's rewards the kinds of jewels and patterns are different. The beauty and honor of New Jerusalem residents are completely different from that of the residents of all other dwelling places of heaven.

Unlike people staying in New Jerusalem, people from other dwelling places of heaven must go through a process to attend the banquet in New Jerusalem. People from the Third, Second, First Kingdoms of Heaven or from Paradise have to change their clothes into the special dresses for New Jerusalem. Since the light of heavenly bodies is different depending on from which dwelling place people come, they have to borrow appropriate clothes to visit dwelling places of a higher level than the place in which they live.

That is why there is a separate place to change the clothes. There are so many dresses of New Jerusalem and the angels help the people change their clothes. Yet, those from Paradise, although there are few, have to change the clothes on their own without the help of the angels. They change their clothes into dresses of New Jerusalem and are deeply moved by the glory of the dresses. They still feel sorry because they are wearing the dresses that they are not really eligible to wear.

People from the Third, Second or the First Kingdoms of Heaven and Paradise have to change their clothes and show the invitations to the angels at the entrance of the banquet hall to enter.

The grand and brilliant banquet hall

When the angels lead you into the banquet hall, you cannot help yourself from becoming overwhelmed by the brilliant lights, the grandeur, and magnificence of the banquet hall. The floor of the hall shines with the color of white gem without any spot or blemish, and it has so many pillars on each side. The round pillars are as clear as glass and the interior is decorated with many kinds of jewels to create this unique beauty. A posy is hanging on each pillar to add to the mood and quality of the banquet.

How happy and overwhelming it would be if you are invited to a ball room that is made of white marble and brilliantly shining crystal! How much more beautiful and happy would the heavenly banquet hall that is made of so many kinds of heavenly jewels be!

At the front of the banquet hall of New Jerusalem, there are two stages that give you a solemn feeling as if you visited back in time and were in attendance of a coronation ceremony of an ancient emperor. At the center of the uppermost stage is a big throne of white gem color for God the Father. On the right of this throne is the throne of the Lord and on the left is the throne of the guest of honor of the first banquet. These thrones are surrounded by brilliant lights and are very high and magnificent. On the lower stage, seats for the prophets are set according to the heavenly rank to express God the Father's majesty.

This banquet hall is big enough to hold countless heavenly citizens invited. On one side of the banquet hall, there is a heavenly orchestra with an archangel as the conductor. This orchestra plays heavenly music to add to the joy and happiness not only during the banquet, but also before the banquet begins.

Being seated with the guidance of the angels

Those who have entered the banquet hall are ushered by the angels to their pre-designated seats, and people from New Jerusalem sit at the front, followed by those who are from the Third Kingdom, the Second Kingdom, the First Kingdom, and Paradise.

Those who are from the Third Kingdom also wear crowns, which are totally different from the crowns of New Jerusalem, and they have to put on round marks on the right side of the crowns to be differentiated from the people of New Jerusalem. Those who are from the Second and First Kingdoms have to put a round mark on their left chest so that they are automatically differentiated from people from the Third Kingdom or New Jerusalem. People from the Second and First Kingdoms wear crowns, but people from Paradise do not have any crowns to wear.

Those who are invited to the New Jerusalem banquet take their seats and wait for the entrance of God the Father, host of this banquet, with a fluttering mind, correcting their clothes and so on. As the trumpet sounds to signal the entrance of the Father, all the people in the banquet hall rise to receive their host. At this time, those who are not invited to the banquet can still partake in the event through simultaneous broadcasting systems installed in their respective dwelling places all around heaven.

The Father enters the hall at the sound of trumpet

At the sound of the trumpet, many archangels who escort God the Father will enter first, and then His beloved forefathers of faith will follow. Now everyone and everything is ready to receive God the Father. The people watching this scene become more eager to see the Father and the Lord, and they fix their eyes to the front.

At last, with brilliant and glorious lights shining, God the Father enters. His appearance is grand and dignified, but at the same time so gentle and holy. His gently waving hair shines in gold, and such bright lights come out from His face and whole body that people cannot even open their eyes properly.

When God the Father comes up to the throne, the heavenly host and angels, the prophets who were waiting on the stage, and all people in the banquet hall bow their heads to worship Him. It is such an honor to see God the Father, the Creator and Ruler of everything, in person as a creature. How joyful and emotional this is! However, not all the guests can see Him. People from Paradise, the First Kingdom and the Second Kingdom cannot lift up their faces because of the brilliant light. They just shed tears of joy and emotion in gratitude for the fact that they can even be at this banquet.

The Lord introduces the guest of honor

After God the Father sits on His throne, the Lord enters ushered by a beautiful and elegant archangel. He is wearing a tall and splendid crown and a shiny, white and long cloak. He looks dignified and is full of magnificence. The Lord bows to God the Father first to be polite, receives the worshipping of the angels, prophets and all other people, and smiles back to them. God the Father sitting on the throne is pleased to be looking at all people attending the banquet.

The Lord goes to a podium and introduces the guest of honor of the first banquet, and in detail tells everything about his ministry that helped finish the human cultivation. Some of the people in attendance at the banquet wonder who it is, or those who already know about him pay attention to the Lord with great expectations.

Finally, the Lord finishes His remarks by explaining how this man loved God the Father, how much he tried to save many souls, and how he wholly accomplished God's will. Then, God the Father is overwhelmed by joy and stands up to welcome the guest of honor of the first banquet, like a father welcoming his son returning home with success, like a king receiving a triumphant general. In the banquet hall filled with expectation and trembling, the trumpet sounds once more and then the guest of honor enters, shining brilliantly.

He is wearing a tall and magnificent crown and a long white cloak like that of the Lord. He also looks dignified but people can feel his gentleness and mercy from his face that resembles God the Father.

When the guest of honor of the first banquet enters, people stand up and begin cheering with their hands lifted as if to form a wave. They turn around and rejoice with others hugging one another. For instance, in the World Cup's final match, when the ball passes by the goal keeper to bring victory, all people of the winner country in attendance or in their homes watching rejoice and cheer, hugging one another, exchanging high-five's, and so forth. Similarly, the banquet hall in New Jerusalem is full of cheers of joy.

Prophets in the First-ranked Group in Heaven

What, then, do we specifically have to do in order to be New Jerusalem residents and attend the first banquet? We not only have to accept Jesus Christ and receive the Holy Spirit as a gift, but also bear the nine fruit of the Holy Spirit and resemble God's heart that is clear and beautiful as crystal. In heaven, the order is decided by the extent to which one is sanctified to resemble God's heart.

Thus, even at the first banquet in New Jerusalem, the prophets enter according to the heavenly rank when God the Father enters the hall. The higher prophets or other forefathers of faith are in the rank, the closer they can stand to God's throne. Similarly, since heaven is ruled in order based on ranking, we know we have to resemble God's heart to stay closer to His throne.

Now let us consider the kind of heart that is clear and beautiful as crystal, like the heart of God and how we can resemble it fully through the lives of the prophets in the first-ranked group in heaven.

Elijah was lifted up without seeing death

Of all the human beings cultivated on the earth, the highest-ranked is Elijah. Through the Bible you can see that every aspect of Elijah's life testified to the living God, the only true God. He was a prophet at the time of King Ahab in the northern kingdom of Israel, where idol-worshipping was rampant. He confronted 850 prophets who worshipped idols and brought down fire from heaven. Elijah also brought a heavy rain after a three-and-a-half-year drought.

Elijah was a man with a nature like ours, and he prayed earnestly that it would not rain, and it did not rain on the earth for three years and six months. Then he prayed again, and the sky poured rain and the earth produced its fruit (James 5:17-18).

Moreover, through Elijah, a handful of flour in a jar and a little oil in a jug lasted until the famine ended. He revived the dead son of a widow and split the Jordan River. In the end, caught in a whirlwind, Elijah went up to heaven (2 Kings 2:11).

What, then, is the reason Elijah, who was the same human being as us, could perform God's powerful works and avoid even death? This is because he accomplished the heart that is as pure and beautiful as crystal that resembles God through many trials during his life. Elijah fully placed his trust in God in any kind of situations and always obeyed Him.

When God commanded him, the prophet went before King Ahab who was trying to kill him and proclaimed that God was the only true God in front of countless people. That is why and how he received God's power, manifested His powerful works so much to greatly glorify God, and came to enjoy honor and glory forever.

Enoch walked with God for 300 years

How about the case of Enoch? Like Elijah, Enoch was also lifted up to heaven without seeing the death. Although the Bible does not mention so much about him, we can still feel how much he resembled the heart of God.

Enoch lived sixty-five years, and became the father of Methuselah. Then Enoch walked with God three hundred years after he became the father of Methuselah, and he had other sons and daughters. So all the days of Enoch were three hundred and sixty-five years. Enoch walked with God; and he was not, for God took him (Genesis 5:21-24).

Enoch began to walk with God at the age of sixty-five. He was so lovely in the sight of God because he resembled God's heart. God communicated with him deeply, walked with him for 300 years, and took him alive to place him close to God Himself. Here, "walking with God" means that God is with that particular person in everything, and God was with Enoch wherever he went for three centuries.

If you go on a trip, with what kind of person would you like to go? The trip will be a pleasant one if you go on it with a person with whom you can share your mind. By the same token, we realize that Enoch was one with God in heart and thus he could walk with God.

Since God is in essence light, goodness, and love, we must not have any darkness in us in order to walk with God but have overflowing goodness and love. Enoch kept himself holy although he was living in a sinful world, and delivered God's will to the people (Jude 1:14). The Bible does not say that he accomplished something great or performed a special duty. Still, because Enoch feared God deep in his heart, avoided evil, and lived a sanctified life to be able to walk with Him, God took him to put him close to Himself more quickly.

Therefore, Hebrews 11:5 tells us, *"By faith Enoch was taken up so that he would not see death; and he was not found because God took him up; for he obtained the witness that before his being taken up he was pleasing to God."* Likewise, Enoch who possessed the kind of faith to please God, was blessed to walk with God always, was lifted up to heaven without seeing death, and became the second ranked person in heaven.

Abraham was called a friend of God

Now, what kind of beautiful heart did Abraham have so that he was called a friend of God and ranked third in heaven?

Abraham fully trusted God and obeyed Him completely. When he was leaving his home country by God's command, he did not even know the destination but in obedience he left his hometown and economic base. Moreover, when he was commanded to offer his son Isaac as a burnt offering, to whom he gave birth at the age of 100, he immediately obeyed. He trusted God who is good and almighty, and who could raise the dead.

Neither was Abraham at all selfish. For example, when his nephew Lot's and his possessions were so great that they were not able to stay together, Abraham let Lot decide first, saying, *"Please let there be no strife between you and me, nor between my herdsmen and your herdsmen, for we are brothers. Is not the whole land before you? Please separate from me; if to the left, then I will go to the right; or if to the right, then I will go to the left"* (Genesis 13:8-9).

On one occasion, many kings united together and invaded Sodom and Gomorrah and seized all the goods and foods as well as his nephew Lot living in Sodom. Then, Abraham took 318 men born and trained in his household, pursued the kings and brought back the goods and food. The king of Sodom wanted to give Abraham some of the restored goods as a token of gratitude, but he declined. Abraham did it to prove that his blessings came only from God. Likewise, Abraham obeyed in faith for God's glory with a heart that is as pure and beautiful as crystal. This is why God blessed him abundantly on this earth as well as in heaven.

Moses, leader of the Exodus

What kind of heart did Moses, leader of the Exodus, have that he is ranked fourth in heaven? Numbers 12:3 tells us, *"Now the man Moses was very humble, more than any man who was on the face of the earth."*

In Jude is a scene in which the archangel Michael disputes with the devil about the body of Moses, and this is because Moses had the qualifications to be lifted up to heaven without seeing death. When Moses was a prince of Egypt, he once killed an Egyptian who was beating a Hebrew. Because of this the devil was blaming that Moses had to see the death.

Yet, the archangel Michael disputed against the devil, saying Moses had thrown away all sins and evil and he had the qualifications to be lifted up. In Matthew 17, we read that Moses and Elijah came down from heaven to have a conversation with Jesus. From these facts we can infer what happened to Moses' body.

Moses had to run away from the palace of Pharaoh because of the murder he had committed. Then, he raised sheep in the desert for forty years. Through the trial in the desert, Moses demolished all his pride, desires, and his own righteousness that he had as a prince in the Pharaoh's palace. Only after that did God assign him the task of bringing the Israelites out of Egypt.

Now Moses, who once killed a person and ran away, had to go back to Pharaoh again and bring out of Egypt the Israelites who had been slaves for 400 years. This seemed impossible by human thought, but Moses obeyed God and went before Pharaoh. Not anybody could be the leader to bring millions of Israelites out of Egypt and lead them to the land of Canaan. That is why God first refined Moses in the desert for forty years and made him a great vessel that could embrace and withstand all the Israelites. In this way, Moses became a person who could obey to the point of death through the trials and could perform the duty of leading the Exodus. We can easily see how great Moses was from the Bible.

Then Moses returned to the LORD, and said, "Alas, this people has committed a great sin, and they have made a god of gold for themselves. But now, if You will, forgive their sin and if not, please blot me out from Your book which You have written!" (Exodus 32:31-32)

Moses knew well that blotting out his name from the book of the LORD did not merely mean physical death. Knowing well that those whose names are not written in the Book of Life will be thrown into the fires of hell, the eternal death, and suffer forever, Moses was willing to take the eternal death for the forgiveness of the people's sins.

What would God have felt looking at this Moses? God was so pleased with him because he thoroughly understood God's heart that hates sin and yet wants to save the sinners; God answered his prayer. God considered Moses alone more valuable than the whole Israelites because he had the heart that was right in the sight of God and was as pure and clear as the water of life originating from His throne.

If there are a bean-size diamond without any blemish or spot, and hundreds of fist-size stones, which would you consider more valuable? No one would exchange a piece of diamond for ordinary stones.

Therefore, realizing the fact that the value of Moses alone, who accomplished God's heart in him, was far greater than that of all the people of Israel combined, we should accomplish hearts that are pure and beautiful as crystal.

Paul, the apostle for Gentiles

The fifth in the heavenly rank is the apostle Paul who devoted his life in evangelizing to the Gentiles. Although he was faithful for God's kingdom to the point of death with so much passion, at one corner of his mind he always felt sorry because he had once persecuted believers of Jesus Christ before accepting the Lord. That is why he confessed in 1 Corinthians 15:9, *"For I am the least of the apostles, and not fit to be called an apostle, because I persecuted the church of God."*

However, since he was such a good vessel, God chose him, refined him, and used him as the apostle for the Gentiles. 2 Corinthians 11:23 onward explains in detail many hardships he suffered while preaching the gospel, and we can see that he suffered so much that he despaired even of life. He was flogged and imprisoned many times. Five times he received from the Jews the forty lashes minus one; three times he was beaten with rods; once he was stoned; three times he was shipwrecked, he spent a night and a day in the open sea; he had often gone without sleep; he had known hunger and thirst and had often gone without food; he had been cold and naked (2 Corinthians 11:23-27).

Paul suffered so much that he confessed in 1 Corinthians 4:9, *"For, I think, God has exhibited us apostles last of all, as men condemned to death; because we have become a spectacle to the world, both to angels and to men."*

Why, then, did God allow so many hardships and persecutions to Paul who was being faithful to the point of death? God could protect Paul from all hardships but He wanted Paul to have a heart as pure and beautiful as crystal through those hardships. After all, the apostle Paul could gain comfort and joy only in God, deny himself completely, and have the perfect form of the Christ. Now he could confess in 2 Corinthians 11:28, *"Apart from such external things, there is the daily pressure on me of concern for all the churches."*

He also confessed in Romans 9:3, *"For I could wish that I myself were accursed, separated from Christ for the sake of my brethren, my kinsmen according to the flesh."* Paul, who had this kind of heart as pure and beautiful as crystal, could not only enter New Jerusalem but also stay close to God's throne.

Beautiful Women in the Sight of God

We have already had a look at the first banquet of New Jerusalem. When God the Father enters the hall, there is a woman behind Him. She is attending God the Father in a white dress that almost touches the floor and is decorated with many kinds of jewels. The woman is Mary Magdalene. Considering the circumstances at that time in which women's public roles were limited, she could not have done so much to accomplish God's kingdom, but because she was such a beautiful woman in the sight of God, she could enter the most revered place in heaven.

Just as there is a rank among the prophets according to how much they resemble God's heart, women in heaven, too, have an order in which they are ranked according to the extent to which they were acknowledged and loved by God.

Then, what kind of lives did such women live to be acknowledged and loved by God and become people of honor in heaven?

Mary Magdalene first met the risen Lord

The woman who is most loved by God is Mary Magdalene. For a long time, she had been bound to the power of darkness and received disdains and contempt from others, and suffered from various diseases. On one of those difficult days, she heard the news about Jesus, prepared an expensive perfume and went before Him. She heard that Jesus had come to the house of one of the Pharisees and went there, but she could not dare to go before Him although she had been longing to meet Him so much. She went behind Him, drenched His feet with her tears, wiped them with her hair, and broke the jar and poured the perfume on Him. She was released from the pains of disease through this act of faith, and she was very thankful. From then on, she loved Jesus so much and followed Him wherever He went, and became such a beautiful woman who devoted her entire life for Him (Luke 8:1-3).

She followed Jesus even when He was crucified and breathed His last, although she knew that her presence alone could claim her life. Mary went beyond the level of merely paying back the grace she had received, but followed Jesus, devoting everything, including her life.

Mary Magdalene, who loved Jesus so much, became the first

person to meet the Lord after His resurrection. She became the greatest woman in the history of mankind because she had such a good heart and beautiful deeds that could even touch God.

The Virgin Mary was blessed to conceive Jesus

The second among the most beautiful women in God's sight is the Virgin Mary, who was blessed to conceive Jesus, who became the Savior for all mankind. About 2,000 years ago, Jesus had to come in flesh to redeem all men from their sins. In order for this to be fulfilled, a woman appropriate in the sight of God was required and Mary, who at the time was engaged to Joseph, was chosen. God let her know beforehand through the archangel Gabriel that she would conceive Jesus by the Holy Spirit. Mary did not involve any human thought but boldly confessed her faith, *"Behold, the bondslave of the Lord; may it be done to me according to your word"* (Luke 1:26-38).

If a virgin became pregnant at that time, she not only had to be disgraced publicly but also stoned to death according to the Law of Moses. However, she believed deep in her heart that nothing was impossible with God and asked it to be done as said. She had a good heart enough to obey God's Word even if it could very well cost her own life. How happy and thankful she would have been when she first conceived Jesus or when she watched Him grow within the power of God! It was such a blessing to happen to Mary, a mere creature.

That is why she was so happy to simply look at Jesus, and she served and loved Him more than her own life. In this way, the Virgin Mary was abundantly blessed by God and received the eternal glory next to Mary Magdalene among all the women in heaven.

Esther did not fear anything for God's will

Esther, who saved her people bravely with faith and love, became a beautiful woman in God's sight and reached the most honorable position in heaven.

After the king of Persia Xerxes took the queen Vashti's royal position away, Esther was selected among many beautiful women and became the queen even though she was a Jew. She s loved by the king and many people because she neither tried to show herself nor was proud, but decorated herself with purity and elegance even though she was already very beautiful.

Meanwhile, while she was in the royal position, the Jews encountered a big crisis. Haman the Agagite, who was favored by the king, was enraged when a Jew named Mordecai did not kneel down before him or pay him respect and honor. Thus, he formed a plot to destroy all Jews in Persia, and received the permission from the king to do so.

Esther fasted for three days for her people and decided to go before the king (Esther 4:16). According to the Persian law at that time, if anybody went before the king without his calling, he or she had to be put to death, except when the king held out his gold scepter to that person. After her three-day fast, Esther relied on God and went before the king with her decision, *"If I perish, I perish."* As a result of God's intervention, Haman, who had conspired, was himself killed. Esther not only saved her people but was also loved all the more by her king.

Likewise, Esther was acknowledged as a beautiful woman and reached the glorious position in heaven because she was strong in truth and had the courage to give up her own life if that were following the will of God.

Ruth had a beautiful and good heart

Now, let us delve into the life of Ruth, who is also acknowledged as a beautiful woman in God's sight and has become one of the greatest women in heaven. What kind of heart and deeds did she have to please God and be blessed?

Ruth the Moabite married an Israelite whose family had moved to Moab because of a famine, but soon lost her husband. All men in her family died early, so she was living with her mother-in-law Naomi and sister-in-law Orpah. Naomi, concerned with their futures, suggested her two daughters-in-law go back to their own families. Orpah left Naomi in tears but Ruth stayed, making an emotional confession as follows:

Do not urge me to leave you or turn back from following you; for where you go, I will go, and where you lodge, I will lodge. Your people shall be my people, and your God, my God. Where you die, I will die, and there I will be buried. Thus may the LORD do to me, and worse, if anything but death parts you and me.

Since Ruth had this kind of beautiful heart, she never thought of her own benefit but only followed the goodness even if it might bring her harm, and did her duty of faithfully serving her mother-in-law with happiness.

Ruth's deed of serving her mother-in-law was so beautiful that the whole village knew of Ruth's fidelity and loved her. Eventually, with the help of her mother-in-law, she got married married to a man named Boaz, a kinsman-redeemer. She gave birth to a son and became the great-grandmother of King David (Ruth 4:13-17). Furthermore, Ruth was blessed to be on the genealogy of Jesus even though she was a Gentile woman (Matthew 1:5-6), and became one of the most beautiful women in heaven next to Esther.

Mary Magdalene Staying Close to God's Throne

What, then, is the reason God is letting us know about the first banquet of New Jerusalem and the order of prophets and women? The God of love does not only want all the people to receive salvation and reach the kingdom of heaven, but also resemble His heart so that they might stay close to His throne in New Jerusalem.

In order for us to receive the honor of staying close to God's throne in New Jerusalem, our hearts have to resemble His heart that is as clear and beautiful as crystal. We have to accomplish the beautiful heart like the twelve foundations of the walls of the City of New Jerusalem.

Therefore, from now on, we are going to delve into the life of Mary Magdalene, who is serving God the Father staying close to His throne. While I was praying for the "Lectures on the Gospel of John," I came to know in great detail about the life of Mary Magdalene through the inspiration of the Holy Spirit. God revealed to me the kind of family into which Mary Magdalene was born, how she lived, and how happy a life she could enjoy after meeting Jesus our Savior. I hope that you will follow her beautiful and good heart to take the blame upon herself in everything and her life-giving love for the Lord so that you too may have the honor of staying close to God's throne.

She was born to an idol-worshipping family

She was named "Mary Magdalene" because she was born in a village called "Magdalena" which was full of idol-worshipping. Her family was not an exception; a curse had fallen upon her family for many generations due to serious idol-worshipping and there were many problems.

Mary Magdalene, who was born in the worst spiritual situation, could not eat properly because of a gastroenteric disorder. Also, because she was physically weak most of the time, her body was vulnerable to all kinds of diseases. Furthermore, even her periods stopped at a young age and she thus lost an important function of a woman. That is why she always stayed in her house and lowered herself as if she were not present. However, even though she was disdained and treated coldly even by her family members, she never had any complaints against them. Instead, she understood them and tried to be a source of strength to them, taking the blame upon herself. When she realized that she could not provide strength to her family members but remained only a burden to them, she left her family. This was not out of hatred or disgust of their maltreatment but only because she did not want to be a burden to them.

Trying her best, taking all the blame on herself

Meanwhile, she met a man and tried to rely on him, but he was such an evil-hearted man. He did not try to support the family but was instead into gambling. He asked Mary Magdalene to bring him more money, often yelling at her and beating her.

Mary Magdalene began needlework while she was searching for a steadier source of income. Still, because she was naturally weak and worked for the whole day, she became even weaker that she had to rely upon somebody else to even move. However, even though the man was being supported by her, he was not even thankful to her but only disregarded her and put her down. Mary Magdalene did not hate him but was instead only sorry that she could not be greater help to that man because of her weak body, and considered all his maltreatment reasonable.

While she was in such a desperate situation, forsaken by her parents, brothers, and the man, she heard very good news. She heard news about Jesus, who performed wondrous miracles such as making the blind see and the mute speak. When Mary Magdalene heard about all these things, she did not have any doubt about the signs and wonders performed by Jesus because her heart was so good. Instead, she had the faith that her weakness and diseases would be healed once she met Jesus.

She longed to meet Jesus with faith. Finally, she heard that Jesus had come to her village and had been staying at the house of a Pharisee named Simon.

Pouring perfume with faith

Mary Magdalene was so happy that she bought perfume with the money she saved from needlework. What must have gone through her emotion upon meeting Jesus cannot be adequately described.

People tried to stop her from approaching Jesus because of her shabby clothes, but nobody could actually stop her passion. Despite people's sharp looks, Mary Magdalene went before Jesus and shed her tears endlessly as she saw His gentle figure.

She could not dare to stand before Jesus, so she went behind Him. When she was at His feet, she shed even more tears and drenched His feet. She wiped His feet with her hair and broke the jar of perfume to pour on them, because to her He was so precious.

Since Mary Magdalene came before Jesus with much earnestness, she was not only forgiven of her sins to reach salvation but also wondrous healing work took place to heal all her internal diseases and her skin disease as well. All her body parts began to function normally again, and she began to have periods. Her face that had looked so awful due to many diseases got filled with joy and happiness and her body that had been very weak became healthy. She found her value as a woman again, no longer bound to the power of darkness.

Following Jesus to the end

Mary Magdalene experienced something for which she was more thankful than healing. It was the fact that she met a person who gave her overflowing love that she had never received from anybody else before. From this time on, she devoted all her time and passion to Jesus with so much joy and gratitude. Because her health was restored, she could support Jesus financially with needlework or other works, and followed Him with all her heart.

Mary Magdalene not only followed Jesus when He performed signs and wonders and changed the lives of many with powerful messages, but was also with Him when He suffered from Roman soldiers and took the cross. Even when Jesus was hung on the cross, she was there. Despite the fact that her presence itself could claim her life, Mary Magdalene went up to Golgotha, following Jesus carrying the cross.

What would she have felt while Jesus, whom she earnestly loved, suffered so much pain and shed all his water and blood?

Lord, what shall I do,
what shall I do?
Lord, how can I live?
How can I live without You, Lord?

...

Only if I could take the blood
You shed,
Only if I could take the pain
You are suffering.

...

Lord,
I cannot live without You.
I cannot live
unless I am with You.

Mary Magdalene did not turn her eyes away from Jesus until He breathed His last, and tried to engrave the glitter of His eye and His face deep inside her heart. Furthermore, she watched Jesus until His last moment and followed Joseph of Arimathea, who put the body of Jesus in a tomb.

Witnessing the resurrected Lord at dawn

Mary Magdalene waited for the Sabbath to pass, and at the dawn of the first day after the Sabbath, she went to the tomb to put perfume on the body of Jesus. However, she could not find His body. She was deeply saddened and wept there, and the resurrected Lord appeared to her. That was how she had the honor to meet the resurrected Lord before anyone else.

Even after Jesus died on the cross, she could not believe this fact. Jesus was her everything and she loved Him so much. How happy she would have been when she met the resurrected Lord in such a dire situation! She could not stop her tears in strong emotion. She did not recognize the Lord at first, but when He called her "Mary" with a gentle voice, she could recognize Him. In John 20:17, the resurrected Lord tells her, *"Stop clinging to Me, for I have not yet ascended to the Father; but go to My brethren and say to them, 'I ascend to My Father and your Father, and My God and your God.'"* Because the Lord also loved Mary Magdalene so much, He showed Himself to her before He met the Father after the resurrection.

Delivering the news of Jesus' resurrection

Can you imagine how uncontrollably happy Mary Magdalene must have been when she met the resurrected Lord, whom she had loved so much? She confessed that she wanted to stay with the Lord forever. The Lord knew her heart, but explained to her that she could not stay with Him for the time being and gave her a mission. She was to deliver the news about His resurrection to the disciples because their minds needed to be settled and comforted after the shock of Jesus' crucifixion.

In John 20:18 we see that *"Mary Magdalene came, announcing to the disciples, 'I have seen the Lord,' and that He had said these things to her.'"* The fact that Mary Magdalene witnessed the resurrected Lord before anyone else and delivered that news to the disciples was not a coincidence. It was the result of all her devotion and service to the Lord with her passionate love towards Him.

If Pilate had asked for anybody who would be crucified on behalf of Jesus, she would have been the first one to say "Yes" and come forth; Mary Magdalene loved Jesus more than her own life and served Him with complete devotion.

The honor of serving God the Father

God was so pleased with Mary Magdalene, who was so good in heart with no evil, and had complete spiritual love. Mary Magdalene loved Jesus with an unchanging and true love since she once met Him. God the Father, who received her good and beautiful heart, wanted to place her close to Him and smell the good and lovely aroma of her heart. That is why, when the time came, He allowed Mary Magdalene to reach the glory of serving unto Him, even touching His throne.

What God the Father wants the most is to gain true children with whom He can share His true love forever. That is why He planned the human cultivation, formed Himself into the Trinity, and has been waiting and withstanding for a very, very long time with human beings on this earth.

Now, when the dwelling places in heaven are all ready, the Lord will appear in the air, and hold the wedding banquet with His brides. Then, He will let them rule with Him for a thousand years and lead them to the heavenly dwelling places. We will live with God the Trinity in utmost happiness and joy forever in heaven that is as clear, pure, and beautiful as crystal, filled with God's glory. How happy the ones who enter New Jerusalem would be since they can meet God face to face and stay with Him forever!

Two thousand years ago, Jesus asked, *"However, when the Son of Man comes, will He find faith on the earth?"* (Luke 18:8) It is very hard to find true faith today.

The apostle Paul, who led the mission of preaching the gospel to the Gentiles, wrote a letter shortly before his death to Timothy, his spiritual son, who was himself suffering from heretic divisions and persecutions on Christians.

> *I solemnly charge you in the presence of God and of Christ Jesus, who is to judge the living and the dead, and by His appearing and His kingdom: preach the word; be ready in season and out of season; reprove, rebuke, exhort, with great patience and instruction. For the time will come when they will not endure sound doctrine; but wanting to have their ears tickled, they will accumulate for themselves teachers in accordance to their own desires, and will turn away their ears from the truth and will turn aside to myths. But you, be sober in all things, endure hardship, do the work of an evangelist, fulfill your ministry. For I am already being poured out as a drink offering, and the time of my departure has come. I have fought the good fight, I have finished the course, I have kept the faith; in the future there is laid up for me the crown of righteousness, which the Lord, the righteous Judge, will award to me on that day; and not only to me, but also to all who have loved His appearing" (2 Timothy 4:1-8).*

If you hope for heaven and long for the Lord's appearing, you have to try to live according to God's Word and fight the good fight. The apostle Paul always rejoiced although he suffered so much while spreading the good news.

Therefore, we must also sanctify our hearts and do our duties more than what we are expected to do to please God so that we can share true love forever staying close to God's throne.

"My Lord,
who is coming
in the clouds of glory,
I long for the day
You will embrace me!
By Your glorious throne,
forever we will share the love
That we could not share on the earth,
and remember the past together.
O! I will go to the heavenly kingdom
in dancing
when the Lord calls me!
O, the heavenly kingdom!"

The Author
Dr. Jaerock Lee

Dr. Jaerock Lee was born in Muan, Jeonnam Province, Republic of Korea, in 1943. In his twenties, Dr. Lee suffered from a variety of incurable diseases for seven years and awaited death with no hope for recovery. One day in the spring of 1974, however, he was led to a church by his sister and when he knelt down to pray, the Living God immediately healed him of all his diseases.

From the moment Dr. Lee met the Living God through that wonderful experience, he has loved God with all his heart and sincerity, and in 1978 he was called to be a servant of God. He prayed fervently so that he could clearly understand the will of God, wholly accomplish it and obey all the Words of God. In 1982, he founded Manmin Central Church in Seoul, Korea, and countless works of God, including miraculous healings and wonders, have been taking place at his church.

In 1986, Dr. Lee was ordained as a pastor at the Annual Assembly of Jesus' Sungkyul Church of Korea, and four years later in 1990, his sermons began to be broadcast in Australia, Russia, the Philippines, and many more through the Far East Broadcasting Company, the Asia Broadcast Station, and the Washington Christian Radio System.

Three years later in 1993, Manmin Central Church was selected as one of the "World's Top 50 Churches" by the *Christian World* magazine (US) and he received an Honorary Doctorate of Divinity from Christian Faith College, Florida, USA, and in 1996 a Ph. D. in Ministry from Kingsway Theological Seminary, Iowa, USA.

Since 1993, Dr. Lee has taken the lead in world mission through many overseas crusades in Tanzania, Argentina, L.A., Baltimore City, Hawaii, and New York City of the USA, Uganda, Japan, Pakistan, Kenya, the

Philippines, Honduras, India, Russia, Germany, Peru, Democratic Republic of the Congo, and Israel. In 2002 he was called a "worldwide pastor" by major Christian newspapers in Korea for his work in the various overseas Great United Crusades.

As of April 2018, Manmin Central Church has a congregation of more than 120,000 members. There are 11,000 branch churches throughout the globe including 54 domestic branch churches, and so far more than 100 missionaries have been commissioned to 26 countries, including the United States, Russia, Germany, Canada, Japan, China, France, India, Kenya, and many more.

As of the date of this publishing, Dr. Lee has written 64 books, including bestsellers *Tasting Eternal Life before Death, My Life My Faith I & II, The Message of the Cross, The Measure of Faith, Heaven I & II, Hell,* and *The Power of God.* His works have been translated into more than 72 languages.

His Christian columns appear on *The Hankook Ilbo, The JoongAng Daily, The Chosun Ilbo, The Dong-A Ilbo, The Munhwa Ilbo, The Seoul Shinmun, The Kyunghyang Shinmun, The Hankyoreh Shinmun, The Korea Economic Daily, The Korea Herald, The Shisa News,* and *The Christian Press.*

Dr. Lee is currently leader of many missionary organizations and associations: including Chairman, The United Holiness Church of Jesus Christ; President, Manmin World Mission; Permanent President, The World Christianity Revival Mission Association; Founder, Manmin TV; Founder & Board Chairman, Global Christian Network (GCN); Founder & Board Chairman, World Christian Doctors Network (WCDN); and Founder & Board Chairman, Manmin International Seminary (MIS).

Heaven I

A detailed sketch of the gorgeous living environment the heavenly citizens enjoy and beautiful description of different levels of heavenly kingdoms.

The Message of the Cross

A powerful awakening message for all the people who are spiritually asleep! In this book you will find the reason Jesus is the only Savior and the true love of God.

Hell

An earnest message to all mankind from God, who wishes not even one soul to fall into the depths of Hell! You will discover the never-before-revealed account of the cruel reality of the Lower Grave and Hell.

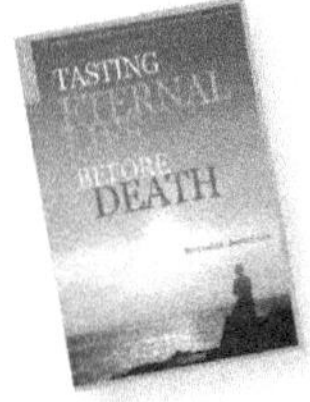

Tasting Eternal Life Before Death

A testimonial memoirs of Dr. Jaerock Lee, who was born again and saved from the valley of death and has been leading an exemplary Christian life.

The Measure of Faith

What kind of a dwelling place, crown and reward are prepared for you in Heaven? This book provides with wisdom and guidance for you to measure your faith and cultivate the best and most mature faith.

Awaken, Israel

Why has God kept His eyes on Israel from the beginning of the world to this day? What kind of His providence has been prepared for Israel in the last days, who await the Messiah?

My Life My Faith I & II

Dr. Jaerock Lee's autobiography provides the most fragrant spiritual aroma for the readers, through his life extracted from the love of God blossomed in midst of the dark waves, cold yoke and the deepest despair.

The Power of God

A must-read that serves as an essential guide by which one can possess true faith and experience the wondrous power of God